Dedication

To the Ones who came before Us, and the Ones yet to come.
To every Black family who has ever made something out of nothing.
To the mothers who stretch dollars, and the fathers who go unseen.
To the ancestors we honor, and the children we protect.
This book is for US.
WE, the RESILIENT.
WE, the REVOLUTIONARY.
WE, the builders of LEGACY.
WE, the deserving of abundant LIFE.
May our names be marked in the annals of history, and our wealth be ever BLESSED, HIGHLY FAVORED &
Forever-ever MULTIPLIED.

CULTIVATE LEGACY

THE BLACK FAMILY'S
GUIDE TO
**LIFE INSURANCE
& GENERATIONAL
WEALTH**

YVETTE BRASWELL

Preface

Cultivate: *To acquire or develop a quality, sentiment, or skill.*
Legacy: *An amount of money, property, influence or values that one passes down to future generations - A gift of will.*
- Merriam-Webster

Getting life insurance is pretty easy. You find a company, talk to an agent and get a policy. It covers your expenses and burial when you pass on. It may even leave some extra money for your family. But cultivating a legacy is different. It's a term that I made to describe a way of putting together life insurance policies that can benefit the owner while they're alive, and also pass down monetary benefits to their beneficiaries or estate when they pass. It's a systematic way of planning for the future, strategizing over time, and intentional money placement that leaves assets for generations. It can be started with very little upfront cash- or a whole lot. Cultivating a legacy is not at all done by accident. But, it's a birthright that is far too often skipped over and undervalued.

Why should you Cultivate Legacy? Simply put, life insurance has an amazing effect on the power of your last name, and how rich or poor your family is in the future. In a perfect world, each generation would be charged with leaving their family better than they found it. The adults would start policies for the babies as soon as they're born, and add on to their wealth (with more assets and policies). Elders would educate the youth on how their family systems work, and make them clear on how they fit into the big picture. Doing these things would create a never-ending cycle of financial growth, leading to more opportunities on all fronts. Unfortunately, this isn't happening enough in disenfranchised communities.

There are many reasons why cultivating legacy is not currently the norm. We're going to get into quite a few of them this book. Life insurance, despite popular belief, is not just about getting buried. When properly done, there would be instructions or a trust in place so that your people know how to use the gifts you've left them. Don't be fooled- You will leave a mark on your family whether you want to or not, because legacy is a gift of WILL. The question is- WILL you leave financial success? Or, WILL you leave poverty, struggle and burden?
Now that we've gotten the formalities out of the way- My name is Yvette Braswell and I am the author of, '**Cultivate Legacy** *(The Black Family's Guide to Life Insurance & Generational Wealth)'*. I wrote this book to help bring clarity, wisdom and assistance with how life insurance works, and how to use it to best serve you/ your family.

Having worked with thousands of customers in my nearly 7 years of experience as a life insurance broker, I've found that when people are well informed and they trust the process, they realize that life insurance is a must-have asset. No matter what place you're currently in financially, I guarantee that there's a way to tailor your policies to affect you and your family's future for the better.

A Few Facts To Consider:
You don't have forever- Nobody knows the day or the hour, but we all have to check out.
You and your family are worthy of a planned inheritance.
You don't need a lot of money to get started.
Coverage at work isn't reliable insurance.
Life Insurance boosts your net-worth by the amount of coverage you have.
It's not hard to do. It's only confusing because you don't know, what you don't know.

I whole-heartedly encourage having a tax-free, NO-Risk, cash accumulating asset to go with your 401k's, IRA's, ABC's & 1-2-3's. In these days and times, we're going to have to be smarter with money than we ever have been before. My hope is that you'll read, re-read, highlight and then DO all of the things. Take swift action with confidence, knowing that you don't have forever to create a path forward. The best time in NOW.

If you have any doubts, questions, comments or observations, you can always reach out to me and my team at www.YvetteBMotivates.com. I'm here to help.

God Bless~~

~Yvette Braswell

Cultivate Legacy

(A Black Family's Guide to Life Insurance & Generational Wealth)

Table of Contents

DISCLAIMER

THIS BOOK IS SOLELY FOR INFORMATIONAL PURPOSES. IT IS NOT LEGAL ADVICE. NOR IS IT INTENDED TO REPLACE THE KNOWLEDGE OF LICENSED AND/OR CERTIFIED PROFESSIONALS. THE PUBLISHER, AUTHOR AND DISTRIBUTORS OF THIS BOOK DO NNOT PURPORT TO BE TAX PROFESSIONALS OR ESTATE ATTORNEYS. IT IS ADVISABLE TO RESEARCH THE APPLICABLE LAWS OF THE APPROPRIATE JURISDICTIONS WHEN CONSIDERING THE INFORMATION.

Introduction

Life Insurance About Family & Finance…

For centuries the story of Black American Wealth has been written without the main character's welfare in mind. What's worse is the American dream has been funded mostly at the expense of people of color- expressly Black people. The price has been paid in blood, sweat and tears- without granting full access to the 'good life'- until this day. However, (especially in this political climate), the time has come for change.

Before I jump into the meat and potatoes of this book, let me give a snapshot of a few things that shape my perspective. I'm an independent life insurance broker of nearly 7 years, who has helped thousands of clients to become insured. In 2019 I came into the insurance game broke, because I had survived a near death health crisis from Endometriosis a few years prior. I was selling any policy that I could- to anybody who thought they wanted coverage. About 6 months into my new career, I too am interest in permanent life insurance. I had gone to a company meeting and heard a speaker talking about how having coverage could both protect people's families and assist in making them wealthy. That was my turning point. From then on, I dedicated my efforts to helping people better understand how their policies could be an asset for them. I knew that a lot of us just simply

didn't get it. Like me, many of my clients had lived their whole lives never having gotten the full story of how life insurance could be used to grow their money and create generational wealth.

Growing up, my folks had done alright. My Mom, a circuit designer and a union representative for Pacific Bell for over 30 years, and my entrepreneur Dad, who owner-operated his beauty salon for decades (which, by the way I inherited at age 19), wanted the very best for my sister and me. Both of them were intelligent and ambitious enough. Plus, we lived in the 80's era of luxury and excess. *Lifestyles of the Rich & Famous/Miami Vice/Dynasty/Different Strokes* had everybody in a chokehold. So, I'm sure that if they knew that they could have made a future of millionaires from the door-to-door insurance man, not only would we be rich- but so would a whole lot of other people we knew. Back then, everybody though insurance was just for making sure you could have a decent burial and leave a lil sump'n to your loved ones. Because that's the information that most adults were working with in those days, they ended up making the best of what they were given.

So anyway, I had spent the better part of four decades in the beauty industry. But, fate found a different way for me to serve my community. A chance meeting, while getting my car serviced, took my life down a completely different path. I met Edford Banuel, who would become my friend and mentor, until this day. I was so green when I started, that for the first 3 months of working, I didn't even realize that my job was in the financial field! Thankfully, even though I was inexperienced, I decided to test a product that not many people were talking about at the time- Index Universal Life Insurance.

Luckily, even a person who knows little to nothing can still thrive. Here's the proof- I got my first IUL policy with only $300 a month in 2019, and grew it to become my first 5-figure legacy! I'm still proud every time I get my little yearly statement. Even as a newbie I was able to do something beneficial for my future. Quiet as it's kept, if I knew then what I know now, I would have put in far more money. The real message here is- If I can do it, I know you can too.

Here's what makes me proud: In spite of our lack of information and our intentional disenfranchisement, Black people have still managed to come a long way in a short time. However, because we've been institutionally discriminated against, we unfortunately still have a long way to go. That's why learning to use life insurance as a financial vehicle (even if you don't fully understand it just yet), is a must. I truly believe that we've all gambled on something with far worse impact than coming up with some accidental cash- (at least once). **Cultivate Legacy** *(The Black Family's Guide to Life Insurance & Generational Wealth*), was born from a truth I could no longer ignore. The tools that create wealth have been hidden from us in plain site for centuries… rarely explained, yet undoubtedly relevant to our financial, sociopolitical and any other conditional term you can think up's- growth. The veil needs to be lifted. We need(ed) education on how to use coverage as a come up- instead of a means to an end- no slight to basic coverage. But, cutting yourself off at the basics is like hearing Stevie Wonders', *Part-Time Lover* and thinking it's the best of his work.

Cultivate Legacy purposely skips over basic burial and cremation coverage and get into one of the easiest, safest and smartest financial tools ever known in building generational wealth. As a broker who now specializes in Index Universal Life and Whole Life with Paid Up Additions insurance, my job is to connect my clients with companies that grow their money and build their family's wealth. Though my niche interest first came out of sheer curiosity of how to make more money (while making my job feel not boring at the same time), next thing I know, I'm paying out-of-pocket to take courses to help move the people towards financial freedom. As I learned more, I saw he difference that sharing makes. I began to see people's retirements, college funds and homeownership savings build. The key to financial success lies in accessibility and the removal of mystery.

Wealth is possible- feasible- and obtainable, when you combine discipline and know how.

This book is not about theory. It contains actionable steps to change your destiny. You'll learn how life insurance can be used to:

- Protect your family with a tax-free lump sum, from the moment you pay your first premium (results vary)
- Grow cash value (as you pay over the years), that can be accessed to fund your dreams
- Work alongside family trusts and estate planning to pass down wealth instead of debt

Life insurance has been quietly used by the world's wealthiest families for protecting their assets, funding their ventures, and passing down way more than just memories- FOR GENERATIONS. The faster Black people can understand the role of a policy and how to leverage it as an asset, the shorter the path to 'The Coin'.

Cultivate Legacy *(The Black Family's Guide to Life Insurance & Generational Wealth),* sheds light on the information that lends opportunities to future generations that our elders never realized was possible. It shows practical steps to put the power of money behind legacy and last name. It explores some historical facts and events that have effected life insurance, and reveals the various ways the socio-political system has excluded Black people. Most importantly, it's going to teach you a few tricks to flipping these policies using time-tested tools.

Thank You for purchasing this book- I hope you use it like your favorite read, or an old cookbook that you love. Come back to it, review, mark up the pages and fill out the information. Pass it on to those you love. Bless a friend with a copy. Let's spread the knowledge like wildfire. Let's build for the generations that we will never touch, or even know in our lifetime. Let's carry the torch for the many voiceless and unseen who paid with their lives, before we were ever thought of.

Let's *Cultivate Legacy.*

P.S.- I will be repeating many of these concepts, so that if you decide to skip over chapters you won't be completely lost.

Chapter 1: What's It All About?

"They put a price on our lives… But they could never dictate our value."

~Cultivate Legacy

The Origin Story

Simply put, a life insurance policy is actually just a contract between you and the financial institution of your choice. On a basic level, it gives your family money when you pass away. A client qualifies for coverage based on age, health, habits and income. They receive protection while alive through a safety net of money and benefits. Most importantly, it shields their family with tax-free money when they pass on, and adds to their net worth while alive.

Many people know that life insurance is important, but we don't always understand why. 56% of Black families have secured coverage, which is much higher than the national average. But, because of our lack of knowledge about how it works, we tend to end our insurance journey before we get to the good part. This is not at all an accident.

A 2021 Barometer study by Life Insurance Marketing and Research Association (LIMRA), shows that 66% of the Black people who own life insurance have only enough coverage to pay for burial costs.

Statistically, people don't want their families to bear the embarrassment of throwing a fish fry or doing a GoFundMe when it's their time to go, (It's so funny how pride can keep a person on the straight and narrow). So, they go on paying premiums for basic coverage that meets little to none of their family's financial needs. I imagine those enslaved Black people who worked for free for 246 years, flipped when they found out their ancestors are still scraping up burial money to this day.

But there's hope yet- In 2025 LIMRA reported that 30% of Black Americans are looking for a financial professional to talk to about maximizing permanent insurance to protect their children and grandchildren. If we continue to work towards normalizing teaching everyone in our families about the true purpose of life insurance, we can reframe its' relationship to ur communities. To unknowingly cheat yourself out of the wealth conversation, because you're not crystal clear about the inner-workings of life insurance, is too heavy a burden to continue to carry.

Let's add some pluses to using life insurance an asset:

- Life insurance is a guaranteed cash benefit for your beneficiaries (the people you leave your insurance money to). If you pay for a $50000 policy, your beneficiaries get $50000 at your passing (even if it happens 1 day after you pay your first premium)
- It adds to your net worth. The sum of all of your policies can be added to your growing investment portfolio. This is great for leveraging when you need to show value to acquire greater assets and loans
- Liquidity- Life insurance builds cash value that can be borrowed and used how you choose while you're alive
- Tax-deferred growth- You don't pay taxes on the cash that you borrow unless you withdraw the cash value. No taxes are charged if you take a loan. You will more than likely put money in your policy that has already been taxed

A Harsh Bit of History:

What most people don't realize is that the modern life industry was built on the backs of enslaved Africans. For well over a century companies like *The Amicable Society for Perpetual Assurance Office* (founded in 1706, England), and *The Nautilus Insurance Company* (which later became *New York Life Insurance*, founded in 1845, America), issued policies on Africans' to their enslavers, who named themselves as beneficiaries. Some of the biggest names in the life insurance industry today- including *New York Life, Aetna, Baltimore Life,* and *AIG* have historical ties to slave insurance policies. These companies built a portion of their fortunes insuring the lives of captive men, women, and children- Giving the people, nor their families, any rights to the death benefits or contracts. Meanwhile, they got *filthy* rich.

From the Middle Passage and sugar cane fields of the Caribbean, to the cotton, rice and indigo fields of the South, human beings died from murder, exhaustion, beatings, starvation, and worse. Insult was added to inhumanities as enslavers received payout after payout without sharing NOT ONE CENT with the 'property' who helped them to fund their livelihoods. There was no dignity, no protection, and no wealth for Black people.

In *The Song Massacre of 1781,* where 132 enslaved Africans were deliberately drowned, by throwing them overboard into the Atlantic Ocean (near Jamaica, allegedly to "save water"). Members of the crew would later try to collect Marine Cargo Insurance from *Lloyd's of London* for their "cargo lost at sea"- aka *HUMAN BEINGS.*

Unsurprisingly, the scar on humanity was that the British court battle following this horrific event was ruled in favor of the human trafficking- shipowners, even though a free African, Olaudah Equine- (a formerly enslaved man), raised his voice in defense of the dead captives. Unfortunately, this was only one of countless assaults and devaluations of Black families at the hands of the system. What's ironic is that an industry that profits daily from "protecting families" was fortified by destroying them.

REFRAME & RECLAIM: From Reaction to Intention

Historically, many Black families have only reactively gotten life insurance- We either buy low value policies after a death in the family. Or, we get insured through work 'benefits' that hold no value (unless you die), only for it to discontinue or become unreasonably expensive once retirement kicks in. We don't realize that choosing to only have the job's coverage is actually giving away the power to set your people up for long-term success. The more brokers, agents and advisors teach these truths, the closer we get to rising above this financial crisis. Life insurance is:

- A financial strategy, not a chore, bill, after-thought or donation
- A tool for the living, not just a plan for the dead and payday for their family
- A safe and secure foundational financial pillar (that never looses money)- Not a frivolous option

What They Don't Want You to Know...

As my father would say, "Ain't nobody doing it, no better than you!". We should know that wealthy families have long used life insurance as a tax-free, recession-proof financial tool. They have many policies that play various roles within their financial portfolio. Those contracts include **Whole Life with Paid-Up Additions, IULs, Annuities** and **Family Trusts.**

American families like the **Rockefellers, Rothschilds, Waltons (Walmart),** and **Disneys** can be useful examples to follow. Like them, we too can fund businesses of mythical proportions, protect family wealth from estate taxes, replace income for future generations, buy estates, educate our children and stay rich for centuries.

Hopefully, as you're reading this book, something in your spirit knows that your family's name was meant for more than survival mode- left broken and invisible. Black people's legacy deserves to be strong as any other community's. Having conversations that are asset/money positive opens doors to upward mobility. We become more than pawns in the financial game.

Chapter 2: Life Insurance at Work~

(May this NEVER be your only coverage)

Why We Need This Conversation

For generations, many people believed that getting a good job and letting their company take care of them was the best way to secure their family's future. Part of that storyline includes employees accepting the low-cost, no living benefits, $100,000 or less, term life insurance policies that their companies offer. Keep in mind that employees are actually paying for this low-value "company" insurance out of their own pockets, (check with your company's HR department to see exactly how much you're paying). The company's "benefits structure" is just temporary comfort shielded under the illusion of safety. And, it literally disappears the moment you clock out for the last time.

In recent years, people are coming to realize that corporate America isn't the once thought of safety net that we were trained to believe. Opening up to acquiring your own life insurance is a way more lucrative practice than having only subpar coverage from an employer. As employees are understanding, more and more, that loyalty too often has been rewarded with limited benefits and borrowed stability, they are choosing to use company insurance as a supplement to the insurance that they buy independently.

Despite the history of the Black community's being systematically directed towards relying on outside resources to direct and dictate our finances, we have always made a way out of no way. **Cultivate Legacy** is helping to further support that shift in mindset, from dependency to design- from reaction to intention. A job paying its employees is one thing. Technically, your job is providing the check to fund your family legacy. But, protecting, creating and building a living legacy- That's a power that lies in you.

In this chapter, we'll uncover four critical reasons why relying on your employer's life insurance could cost your family everything. And, why buying your own coverage is one of the smartest and most liberating financial moves you'll ever make.

Wealth-building through life insurance is about the long game. Your policy is an asset, because it gains value over time. You can leverage it to get loans and buy more assets. Your job, is to structure your asset to not only pay for your burial, leave money to your loved ones and pay off big-ticket bills when you pass- but also to accumulate interest so you can retire on your own terms and pay for important landmark events in you and your people's lives. When you carefully plan your financial structure with a life broker, your income can continue to grow and protect your family long after the job's paychecks stop coming.

Let's break down reasons why owning your own life insurance policy is a non-negotiable, if you're serious about building wealth.

1. You're Paying for Insurance You'll Never Own

Most people think on the job life insurance is free. It is absolutely not. The company takes your money right out of your paycheck each month to pay for it. You're literally paying for a benefit that will go away when you leave the company. Your employer's goal isn't to build you or your family's wealth, but to offer you the bare minimum required to look competitive with other corporations. Companies often offer coverage equal to one or two times your salary, which sounds good until you realize how little that actually provides for your family after debts and funeral expenses. This can work as an addition to your self-insurance, but is not recommended as a stand alone practice.

2. It's Cheap Now- But You Pay Down The Line

You may not realize it. But your job could quite possibly be making you waste time and money on one of your most precious wealth building tools. Your employer-provided coverage is called *group life insurance*- meaning the employer owns multiple policies for all its employees- even though the employees are paying for them. Simply put, group life insurance covers employees under no-nonsense plans with no living benefits or cash accumulation. And, the insurance usually only lasts while a person is employed. Once they leave the company (whether they quit, get laid off, or retire), that coverage usually ends immediately- protection is lost, and the employees are left uninsured. They are responsible to either find a new job that offers that same level of insurance, or try to qualify for a policy of their own. By the time the employee understands what's going on, years that could have been spent growing cash value and benefits in a self-owned policy are lost. As a result, many ex-employees end up having to buy unnecessarily expensive insurance, they end up older and under insured, or with no coverage at all.

3. Why You Need Your Own Insurance Before You Retire

You see how I keep repeating that retiring without personal coverage in place is a huge mistake for you and your family? There's a reason… Trying to buy your own policy after age 60 or 65 makes your premiums skyrocket to an astronomical increase of at least 86% more than you would have at age 30- young working age (Source: Value Penguin by Lending Tree). God forbid your health has changed even slightly! You might not qualify for any coverage at all. If you take nothing else from **Cultivate Legacy,** take this:

PLEASE BUY YOUR FAMILY'S OWN LIFE INSURANCE WHILE YOU'RE YOUNG AS POSSIBLE, HEALTHY AND INSURABLE.

It locks in a lower monthly payment, gives you full control over your policy, and gives you the opportunity to make a cash value producing asset with very little effort.

4. Real Security Comes From Ownership

Owning your own life insurance policy gives you:

- Portability- You take it wherever life leads you
- Control- You decide/design how much coverage you want, how much value you want to build and how long you want it for
- Access- You can borrow from your policy's cash value with no credit check, age limitations, or permission while you're alive. And, it usually arrives in your bank account within 48 hours. You're in charge
- Peace of mind- You know that you and your family are cash-strong with protection that no company, boss, or job can take it away

Final Thoughts

Your Job Is Temporary- But Your Legacy Is Forever

A job can end. But your family's needs will not. So, let's make a pact: *We don't rely on anyone (who hasn't consulted with us first), to make the financial decisions for the most important people in our lives.*
Not choosing how you want to be protected is too close to letting your boss design you and your family's future. The power to decide your retirement, your children's college funds, or even how much money you want to nest away is totally up to you. Protecting your legacy on your own terms is always the better choice- even if it cost a few extra dollars.

Chapter 3: What Are Living Benefits?

Most people think of life insurance as something that helps only after they're gone. But, not you my dear. You're learning to structure the right policies to move you and yours into the future you're designing while you're alive. This is why understand living benefits is super important.

Living benefits turn your life insurance into a lifeline- a source of tax-free funds that can help you survive, recover, and rebuild before your family ever needs the death benefit. It's one of the most powerful, and most overlooked, parts of modern life insurance.

What Exactly Are Living Benefits?

Living benefits are features (or "riders"), built into many life insurance policies that allow you to access a portion of your death benefit early, if you experience certain medical conditions or life events. Some riders come with the policy, while others have to be paid for separately. We're going to discuss a few of the most common free living benefits.

They're typically triggered by three categories:

1. Terminal Illness

If you're diagnosed with a terminal illness and a doctor certifies that your life expectancy is typically 12-24 months or less, you can access part of your death benefit right away.

How it helps:

Pays for care, treatment, or home modifications

- Alleviates stress during a very critical time, because the policy owner/insured has access to up to 80% of the death benefit when it's most needed
- Allows for focusing on quality time with loved ones
- Settles affairs while you're still able to make decisions

Example: *If you have a $500,000 policy, you may be able to access up to $400,000 while you're still living, leaving the remainder for your beneficiaries later.*

2. Chronic Illness

A chronic illness benefit helps when the insured can no longer perform at least two everyday tasks without help. Once a doctor confirms that you need assistance with your Activities of Daily Living (ADLs), like bathing, dressing, eating, or walking for 90 days or more, your policy may allow you to access part of your benefit- monthly or as a lump sum.

How it helps:

- Pays bills while the insured is off work or waiting for workman's compensation or disability benefits to kick in
- Pays for in-home care or assisted living
- Covers medical equipment or family caregiving costs
- Maintains dignity and independence without draining savings

Key features to know:

- You can usually take between 2% to 4% of your death benefit per month. For example, if your policy's death benefit is $100,000 and the company allows you 3% per month, that would be $3000 per month to help towards your monthly expenses
- Funds can be used however you choose- not just for medical bills
- It's recommended to repay the loan that is borrowed from the policy, but it's not mandatory. In the end, the death benefit on the policy will be minus whatever amount (plus fees), that has been borrowed and not repaid

Example: *A $300,000 policy might pay $9,000 per month for up to 33 months if you become chronically ill.*

3. Critical Illness

Critical illness riders pay out if you experience life-altering medical events- like a heart attack, stroke, cancer diagnosis, or organ transplant.

How it helps:

- Provides fast cash to cover medical bills and lost income
- Prevents you from going into debt or dipping into retirement funds
- Keeps your household afloat during recovery

Common covered conditions include:

- Heart attack
- Stroke
- Major organ transplant
- End-stage renal failure
- Cancer (invasive or late stage)
- Paralysis or severe burns

Example: *If you survive a heart attack and your $250,000 policy allows for 50% critical illness access, you could receive $125,000 (in total), tax-free to cover recovery expenses or replace your income.*

Living Benefits by Policy Type

Here's how living benefits function across different types of life insurance policies:

Term Life Insurance

- Includes accelerated benefit riders for terminal, chronic, or critical illness

- Limited flexibility- once the term ends, so does the benefit
- No cash value or savings component (a few exceptions)
- Great for low-cost, temporary protection but not long-term wealth planning

Whole Life Insurance

Provides lifetime coverage with guaranteed cash value growth

Includes terminal illness and accidental death riders

Allows the policy owner to borrow against cash value tax-free

The owner can borrow cash and the death benefit early if they become ill

**Accidental death gets an honorable mention with whole life. Though it's not free, it's a great way to double or triple a whole life policy's death benefit, depending on how the insured person passes away. Accidental death can also be purchased as a stand alone policy that's great for people under 45-50 years old who medically can't qualify for a standard life insurance policy.*

Indexed Universal Life (IUL)

Offers the broadest flexibility and growth potential

Cash value grows based on interest rates marked by stock market performance (without the risk of loss)

Living benefit often include chronic, critical, and terminal illness

Allows tax-free income access through policy loans (not withdrawals), in retirement

Why Living Benefits Matter- You Can:

- Avoids financial devastation during illness or recovery
- Maintains control over how and when your benefits are used. And, acts in addition to any other benefits you may have in place
- Preserves your family's inheritance instead of spending it on medical bills
- Allows the insured to live with dignity, independence, and financial peace of mind

Knowing how the game goes is half the battle. With living benefits, your policy becomes a tool for protection, stability, recovery, and freedom.

Chapter 4: Insurance Strategy

(How to use life insurance like the wealthy)

Why This Chapter Matters

Assets: A resource with economic value that an individual or organization owns or controls… Items of value that can be used to generate revenue or be converted into cash". (Investopedia)

The wealthy have been playing the insurance game for centuries. And, though Black people became customers way later down the line, we still have action at cutting out a lane for ourselves with the various types of policies and family trusts.

In this chapter we'll walk through the strategies behind some of the wealthiest people's fortunes in America, and learn how to mix and match their blueprints to create something tailor made especially for you.

Note: It's very important to normalize having a life insurance budget. The current best practice is to split 10%-15% of your monthly income between your policies. This allows you to have a reasonable, maintainable budget. So if you catch a flat, your water heater busts, or when an emergency comes (which is inevitable), you won't be canceling your legacy plans, because you can no longer afford them. The budget makes space for your life insurance portfolio to build as your family fortune to grows.

How the Rockefeller Family Used Life Insurance to Build an Infinite Family Bank

Let's start with The Rockefellers- one of America's richest families (net worth over $10 billion). They were famous for using **Whole Life** policies paired with irrevocable trusts on multiple family members to create a "family bank" system^**.

The Rockefellers took out permanent life insurance on every family member, and named their irrevocable trust as the beneficiary of the policies^*. This move safeguarded that funds from their insurance policies had instructions and rules attached to how they should be used and allocated. This helped to both preserve and grow their family legacy. When the time came to buy real estate, fund ventures, pay for taxes, education and charities, they already had wealth accumulated. This method of layering assets is know as the "waterfall method". It works because each time a family member passes away, their death benefit goes into the trust. The process helps pay off loans on debts and other policies, while activating funds towards new policies for future generations. Money circulates decade after decade, which is why their name and legacy is so influential. Something to think about: *Why hand down just assets, when you could pass down a legacy with heavily accumulated cash value?*

The Rockefellers' waterfall method is a proven estate tax-proof, lawsuit-proof and even bad market-proof system. The best part is that it can be repeated, generationally, over-and-over again. Consider this- their family didn't even have access to **Index Universal Life** (IUL), policies when they began the waterfall method. Can you imagine how much more they would have been worth than $10 billion with a no-cap interest rate for over 100 years?

You Can Use Rockefellers' Method:

- **Step 1: Meet with an Estate Lawyer** and set up a Trust in order to get the full benefits from the policies (Irrevocable Life Insurance Trust or family trust), which will help avoid estate taxes and ensures payouts are distributed based on your family's legacy plan
- **Step 2: Take out IUL and/or Whole Life policies** on yourself, your children, and/or grandchildren with a broker that uses A-rated life insurance and mutual life companies that pay dividends

- **Step 3: Add Paid-Up Additions (PUAs)** to grow the cash value of your **Whole Life** policy faster, as you increase future death benefits for your beneficiaries
- **Step 4: Name your trust as the beneficiary** of your family's policies, instead of a person, which allows funds to be held, protected, and used for defined purposes (college, homes, business capital, etc.)
- **Step 5: Use policy loans** (NOT WITHDRAWLS), to fund family investments without ever needing to ask a bank or have your credit approved.

Result: Your family members will never have to start building wealth from scratch. Your capital stays safely in-house. Your assets are preserved, not sold.

How Walt Disney Used Life Insurance to Fund a Dream

Can you imagine how hard it must have been for Walt Disney to try and convince the banks to invest in a cartoon mouse and duck themed amusement park???

This man really had to have some cojones! As it turns out, banks never believed in Walt Disney's vision- Well, at least not at first. Thank goodness for cash-value **Whole Life** policies!

When Walt Disney couldn't get funding for Disneyland, he decided to take a cash value loan from his own life insurance policy to fund his dream. This was possible solely because his **Whole Life** coverage had built liquidity over time.

In 1954, when Walt Disney couldn't get funding from banks to build Disneyland, he took a $60000 cash loan from his Whole Life insurance policy to finance the early stages of his project. Disney's loan only charged him a 2% interest rate to borrow money from HIMSELF and pay HIMSELF back***.

As it turns out- Disneyland HIT! It opened in 1955, and attracted 3.6 million guests in its first year. To date, the cartoon mouse and duck have hosted more than 700 million people from all over the world. It always pays to have your own 'yes' in your back pocket when the rest of the world is telling you 'no'.

The Moral: Getting a cash value policy is never a bad idea, because who better to fund your dreams than you?

P.S. Believe in yourself. Bet on yourself. DO YOU.

How You Can Apply It:

- **Step 1: Choose a Whole Life** or **IUL** policy with strong cash value growth.
- **Step 2: Overfund the policy** (with PUAs for Whole Life or additional premium payments for **IUL's**), to accelerate liquidity in the early years whenever possible.
- **Step 3: Dump a Lump Sum into your policy first whenever possible.** Then, when you want to use your cash

value to buy a big ticket item or to invest in an asset that you've been saving for, you have the option to do it. Clients that make monthly payments to go along with their initial lump sum payments have a greater chance at taking advantage of how market growth will affect their cash value. After 3–5 years (with an IUL), you'll begin to see the accessible cash value accumulate. With Whole life, you have immediate (within 30 days), access to borrow against cash value to fund your projects without credit checks, income verification, or any repayment schedules. YOU set the rules for your asset. However, if you decide to pay yourself back (which is highly recommended), it will bubble your cash value and help to compound your interest.

- **Step 4: Make monthly payments into your permanent life insurance policy** (even if you don't have a lump sum). After 3–5 years, you'll really begin to see the accessible cash value accumulate. If you have an IUL, it's recommended to allow your policy to grow for 10-15 years before you touch the cash value. Why, you ask? You want to give the high interest rate attached to an IUL a chance to really go to work for you. The more money you put in, the greater the difference that every year of interest can make. Then, when you've let your policy properly marinate, you can borrow against it free and clear. Again, when you decide to pay yourself back, it will greatly increase your cash value and compound interest further.

- **Step 5: Use policy loans to fund:**
  - ■ Real estate down payments or projects
  - ■ Startup costs for your business
  - ■ Equipment, marketing, expansion, or staff
  - ■ ASSETS THAT WILL GENERATE MONEY FOR YOU TO PAY OFF YOUR SELF-LOAN

Step 6: REPAY THE LOAN TO YOURSELF- I Can't Repeat Enough. It's totally on your terms. The person who's savvy about their business knows to add a little extra to cancel out the fees that the life insurance company will charge for doing the transaction. We don't need the death benefit payouts to be reduced by the amount of money owed

Result: You don't have to liquidate your investments or borrow from a traditional bank. You become your own source of capital.

Ray Kroc- McDonalds Franchise Founder Used Insurance As A Source Of Capital

Ray Kroc was a man on a mission to take his business from being a local hamburger stand to being a household staple in the food industry. And, this man had dogged determination. Since traditional financing wasn't available to a 52 year-old Ray, he borrowed against his permanent life insurance policy to buy his business. For 8 years he never even took a personal salary*. He used his accumulated cash value to pay for his infamous 'Golden

Arches' campaign. He even borrowed against his policies to keep his key employees paid. However, because Ray Kroc didn't need credit or collateral to take out tax-free loans from his policies, he was able to design the terms of his success. He bought his first McDonalds franchise in Des Plaines, Illinois in 1955, and later bought out Dick and Mac McDonald in 1961.

Ultimately, Mr. Kroc grew more than 700 restaurants within 10 years, from two permanent cash value life insurance policies.**

Ray Kroc knew where to put his money. He bet on himself in a winning industry, creating an amazing asset with returns can't even be counted- I mean, *c'mon- It's McDonalds!*

How You Can Apply It:

- **Step 1: View your life insurance policy as a long-term liquidity reserve.** Overfund it whenever you can by paying extra (with awareness to MEC rules, so you don't get into tax trouble), each month or to build significant cash value early
- **Step 2: Use your reserve cash value to make strategic, low-risk moves** (e.g., purchase discounted real estate, buy into family-owned property, or fund a renovation)
- **Step 3: Grow your wealth externally while your policy continues to grow internally** (SAVE some cash- then intentionally put that money where it works for you, instead of vice versa)
- **Step 4: Create your own version of a Family Office** by making your own "waterfall method", where the family's

capital makes its' own wealth. Make your money, then buy insurance and direct the death benefits to go back into the family trust. The family office instructs how cash from policies should be used, how loans are repaid, and how death benefits should be reinvested or redistributed. As always, you make the terms for what wealth looks like for your family

Result: You turn your premium payments into legacy tools that give you access to opportunity and wealth, not just protection.

Using Life Insurance for Tax-Free Payouts

When structured correctly, life insurance benefits are income tax-free under IRS Code §101. Here's how to ensure it stays that way:

- Always list **beneficiaries** on your policy (do not leave the payout to your estate)
- Whenever possible, add a **contingent beneficiary** (if you're not naming your family trust as the beneficiary)
- Avoid **policy loans** exceeding 90% of your cash value, unless you plan to repay your policy right back
- Consider using an **Irrevocable Life Insurance Trust (ILIT)** if your estate value may be over the federal estate tax threshold (especially important in high-net-worth families)
- Keep policies in force and paid up so the contract doesn't lapse and trigger **taxable gains**

Bonus: Loans against the policy are not taxable because you're borrowing against your own asset, not withdrawing or cashing it out.

Why Permanent Life Insurance Doesn't Depend on Market Volatility

- **Whole Life** policies offer guaranteed growth and are backed by the insurance company's general account, which is typically invested in high-grade bonds and other conservative assets.
- **Indexed Universal Life (IUL),** policies grow based on the performance of a stock index (like the S&P 500), but with a floor (usually 0%)- Meaning your money is protected and you never lose, when the market drops or experiences a loss for the year. In other words, life insurance is one of the safest ways to protect your money from diminishing, because it doesn't expose your money to risk.
- In both policies, your money is safeguarded from market downturns, making this method of asset protection attractive during recessions or periods of inflation.

Final Thoughts

We don't need to wait to become millionaires/billionaires before we begin using the same strategies the wealthy have used since insurance game was invented. We can move with the same intentionality, education, and consistency of the Rockefellers. We can be as brave as Walt Disney, or as determined as Ray Kroc.

Once you realize that you're building stability, security, and opportunity with every premium you pay, life insurance no longer feels like a chore. It becomes not only your privilege, but one of your greatest allies. Just keep in mind that it's okay if you don't have a lot of extra cashflow when you start. The most important thing is to begin wherever you are, and grow in the discipline of putting money into assets that give you future goals to work towards. Build your empire from the ground up on your own timeline.

Having the understanding of why it's important to get your own coverage, and how living benefits work in your favor- it's now time to learn how to shape your policies to fit your legacy. You're ready to Insure like it's Couture!

Go to www.yvettebmotivates.com for help with creating your family insurance strategy

^* Source: FWD *www.fwd.com.ph*, *'The Rockefellers' Life Insurance Blueprint for Perpetual Wealth'*, Forward Life Philippines

Source: *www.BankingTruths.com, 'How Walt Disney Used Whole Life As His Own Bank Long Before IBC Was A Thing'*

**Source: *www.CaryleVinson.com, 'How McDonalds Was Founded with Life Insurance!'*, July 16, 2021

*** Source: *www.commercebank.com, 'The Story Of The Loan That Helped Build Disneyland'*, October 20, 2021

Chapter 5: Filling the Gap

(Building What Has Been Denied)

Though LIMRA research shows that Black Americans are more likely to own life insurance than any other race, the reality is that 46% (20 million adults), are un/under insured. This has made a significant wealth gap in the Black community- one rooted in enslavement, fueled by marginalization and steeped in racism. Our current relationship with insurance is a reflection of the systematic divide that has been orchestrated between Black families and other racial groups, for centuries in America. Our situation is a direct result of hundreds of years of policies, intentional exclusion and barriers that either deny or give bare bones access to wealth, land, loans and investments.

This chapter will give clarity to who did what. When we understand the reasons behind the gap, we can put ourselves in a better position. By choosing life insurance based on our needs, values, and long-term visions, we can start to narrow the divide. Let's take a look at some statistics and explore:

- How the wealth gap was engineered
- What our current economic standing looks like
- How we can use life insurance to intentionally close the gap
- And why we must shift the focus from spending to legacy-building

Systems That Separated Us From Wealth

Here is a peek into the systems that America put in place to maintain the financial oppression of Black people:

- Homestead Act (1862): Gave White settlers 270 million acres of public land free and clear, for a small filing fee (of about $18), only requiring them to live for 5 years and cultivate or improve their plot of land. Blacks, Natives and Confederate supporters were expressly excluded.
  Source: California Trail Interpretive Center, The Homestead Act of 1862
- GI Bill (1944): Enacted after World War II to aid returning veterans in their transition back to civilian life. The GI Bill provided education, vocational training, unemployment compensation, home loan guarantees and access to various healthcare benefits- majorly to the White veterans. This bill

helped to establish America's middle class. However, Black veterans were routinely denied access to housing and benefits.

Source: National Archives (.gov), Servicemen's Readjustment Act of 1944

Result: Access to land and home ownership means that the average White family is now twice as likely to receive 3 times as much inheritance as Black families (Economic Policy Institute).

Redlining: Officially began in the 1930's, blocking Black families from homeownership and generational equity, until it was officially outlawed in 1968. By denying Black families access to mortgages and other financial services, it hindered our abilities to build wealth and equity through homeownership. The consequences of redlining has contributed to higher poverty rates, limited access to financial services and neighborhood decline within Black communities. Its' effects continue to be felt across generations, directly affecting upward mobility.

Source: National Institutes of Health, Modern Day Consequences of Historic Redlining: Finding a Path Forward

Result: Lack of access to generational wealth puts Black families at the bottom of the wealth and income lists.

- **Estate and inheritance laws:** Historical estate and inheritance laws have significantly impacted the Black community, primarily through the issue of **heirs' property.**

This refers to land passed down through generations without a clear legal title, due to a lack of wills and trusts. The absence of proper paperwork was a combination of historical factors including ineligibility for loans and programs, forced sales, and hinderance to urban development due to complexities around ownership. Without proper preparation or access to legal, financial and insurance tools, many Black families passed down debt instead of assets. This has had an enormous negative effect on the Black community.

Source: Land Trust Alliance Resource Center, 'History of Heirs' Property

Result: Only 43% of Black Americans own their own homes.

- **The Welfare System:** Created in 1935, the U.S. Welfare System expanded rapidly by the 1960s and 70s. While it provided temporary relief for many, its' conditions especially harmed the Black family structure. Men were disqualified from the household in order for women and children to receive benefits. This established economic incentives for families to separate. Over time, it contributed to generational cycles of fatherlessness, crime, underemployment, and limited wealth transfer. This was policy that created long-term consequences affecting Black people to this day.

Source: Social Welfare History Project- Virginia Commonwealth University, 'Aid To Dependent Children'

Average household wealth by race:

Group	Median Household Wealth
White	~$250,400
Asian	~$535,400
Latino	~$48,720
Black	~$24,520

Source: US Census, 2025

Our Spending Power vs. Our Wealth
Painful Truths:
Black Americans have over $1.98 trillion in annual spending power, yet hold less than 15% of the wealth of the average household.

- We are top consumers in beauty, fashion, cars, and tech.
- Only 22% of Black families own investment accounts.

- Only 31% of Black families have a will in place.
- Less than 60% have any life insurance at all- and most of those are small value term policies, as opposed to wealth-building contracts.

Source: Investor's Business Daily Source: Legal Zoom/Caring.com, 2023

Closing The Gap: From Targets To Triumphant

****When considering your life insurance budget, it's good practice to split 10%-15% of your monthly income between your policies. As your income grows, you grow your insurance portfolio. Lump sum deposits affect the speed of executing your plan.*

Mending the Effects of the Homestead Act of 1862 (Land Theft & Exclusion)

The Homestead Act gifted White Americans stolen 'free land', creating automatic wealth for millions of households while excluding Native and Black families. Today, the goal is simple- **CREATE YOUR OWN LAND FUND.**

Actionable Steps- Start small~ The goal is ownership, not perfection.

- **Step 1: Open a Whole Life or IUL Policy Immediately**
  - If money is tight: start with **$50–$150/month**
  - If you can afford more: **$150–$300 and up /month** grows faster

- ■ Get comfortable with saving the bulk of your money in your permanent life insurance where you have exponential interest and almost immediate access to take a loan

- **Step 2: Make this your "Property Down Payment Fund"**

After approx. 7-10 years of monthly payments, your cash value becomes your:

- ■ Full payment for a Homestead Property
- ■ Down payment for construction or land purchase
- ■ Down payment for a duplex, multi-unit, empty lots in growing areas, property in developing areas, commercial property or a home with potential income property attached

- **Step 3: Borrow Against the Policy (NEVER Withdraw)**

Loans do NOT require:

- ■ CREDIT CHECKS
- ■ JOB HISTORY
- ■ BANK APPROVAL

YOU ARE YOUR OWN BANK.

Reverse the GI Bill Exclusion (Education & Business Capital)

Black veterans were blocked from low-interest loans and college access.

Today, you can create your own version of the GI Bill with your policy.

Your Action Plan

Step 1: Open an IUL for Each Child (or Grandchild)

- Start with **$25–$50 and up/month** for babies (ex. $60 per mo. = approx. $15000 by age 18)
- **$50–$100 and up/month** for teens (ex. $85 per mo. at 16 yo. = approx. $15000 by age 30)
- **$100–$300 and up/month** for adults (ex. $200 per mo. at 35 yo. = approx. $15000 by age 45)

Step 2: Designate Life Events for Future Withdrawals or Loans

Cash value can be used for:

- College tuition
- Trade school
- A first business
- Certifications
- Down payment on a first home

Step 3: Teach Your Heirs the Purpose of the Policy

- Start their IUL policies as soon as the children bust out the plastic! If you can't do that, get it done ASAP

- Normalize teaching children the importance of saving money in a high yield life insurance policy as a means to have a future full of wealth, for generations to come
- The best money is unseen

Create a simple rule:

"If you borrow from this policy, you must use it for an asset, NOT a liability."
No shoes.
No vacations.
No sections/bottle service.
No cars that depreciate.

Only:
- Businesses
- Education
- Property
- Investments

Voila! You just created a GI (Generational Independence) Bill.

How to Reverse the Impact of Redlining (Banking & Credit Discrimination)

Redlining blocked mortgages and financial services from Black families.

Life insurance gives you BANK-INDEPENDENT capital, so you never have to beg a lender.

Your Action Plan

Step 1: Build Cash Value Intentionally

- **Split 10%-15% of your monthly income between your policies**
- IUL: At least **$150–$300/month. Ages 50 and above $300 and up**
- Whole Life with PUAs: **$100–$250/month**

(If you can't start at these numbers, begin with less (the key is CONSISTENCY)

Step 2: Use Cash Value for These Moves ONLY

- Buying a home
- Buying rental property
- Starting a business
- Paying down high-interest debt
- Emergency safety net

Step 3: Use Policy Loans Instead of High-Interest Banks

Loan interest from your policy goes BACK INTO YOUR POLICY, not to the bank.

This is how you:

- Escape predatory lenders

- Improve your credit
- Build equity
- Stay liquid during financial emergencies

The only Reds we're acknowledging are Detroit Red, Redd Foxx and Sexxy Red.

How to Reverse Estate & Inheritance Losses

Black families have lost billions because were systematically left out of the historical conversation in the wealth game. Life insurance provides guaranteed liquidity that PROTECTS the estate. Historically:

- We are un/under insured, AND are directed towards getting policies that usually don't add to the value of our legacy
- We don't have wills
- We don't have trusts
- Our heirs fight
- Probate drains our wealth
- Property gets sold instead of kept

Your Action Plan

Step 1: Open a Whole Life Policy for Legacy Purposes

- Start with as much money as is feasible every month for the policy premium. Using a portion of your saving or a lump sum of money is a great way to kickstart your plan. 5%-7% of your income each month is recommended. You can always grow

- Keep expanding your vision by maxing out the monthly payment allowed by your insurance carrier, because this grows the cash value that you will use to build your legacy
- Name your trust as the beneficiary once it's created

Step 2: Create a Simple Trust (Budget-Friendly Options)

If you cannot afford a lawyer yet use:

- **Trust & Will** ($400–$600)
- Or **Nolo** ($60–$80)
- www.doyourownwill.com (Free)
- **Irrevocable Trust** through an estate planner later ($750-$3500)

Step 3: Title These Items in Your Trust

- Your home
- Your secondary property
- Your bank accounts
- Your life insurance policies
- Your business interests

Step 4: Choose a Responsible Trustee (Not your most emotional family member.)

Choose someone who:

- Pays bills on time
- Is organized
- Understands your values

Step 5: Review the Trust Every Year

- Update for:
- New babies
- New property
- Changed relationships
- New financial goals

How to Counter Systemic Racism Overall

Life insurance creates a **private, non-discriminatory financial system** for your family.

It cuts out the predators and removes gatekeepers, replacing them with structure, intention, and math.

Your Action Plan

Step 1: Create a 3-Policy Wealth Stack

This is your family's private financial system:

1. **Term-** covers income & large expenses for a limited timeframe. The cash-back option is best if term is your choice
2. **IUL-** builds long-term tax-free retirement & cash access
3. **Whole Life w/ PUAs-** funds your trust & anchors your legacy with a solid cash value growth insurance policy that gives you instant access to use the accumulate money

The Sky Is The Limit- Yet even on a small, steady budget success can be formed:

- Term: **$20–$40/month**

- IUL: **$75–$150/month**
- Whole Life: **$50–$100/month**

Step 2: Implement the Family Rule

No one buys a liability without first buying an asset

Step 3: Hold Annual Family Wealth Meetings

Topics:

- Location of policies
- Access instructions
- Trustee roles
- Financial lessons
- Goals for next year

Step 4: Create a Family Vault

Digital or physical folder that stores:

- Policies
- Bank info
- Trust docs
- Passwords
- Deeds
- Final wishes

Final Thoughts

Now that we know how Black people have been systematically left behind in America's wealth plan, it's important to be intentional about putting life insurance in place for family members as early as possible. The wealth gap didn't happen by accident- it was engineered through laws and economic systems that deliberately shut Black families out of land ownership, affordable housing, capital access, inheritance structures, and financial protection. However- the same financial tool that was once weaponized against us is now one of the most effective, accessible, and predictable ways to be used in rebuilding what was stolen.

Life insurance is a tool in which powerful, steady and independent additions to policies can swiftly add to financial portfolios and net worth. Well structured **Term, Whole Life,** and **IUL** policies are the vehicles to drive a way off of the bottom of the economic list. Black people can take a portion of that $1.98 trillion in annual spending and work with skilled insurance specialists to empower communities.

We cannot rewrite history- But we can author what happens next.

Permanent life insurance allows Black families to:

- Self-fund education
- Buy land and property
- Start businesses

- Protect assets from courts and creditors
- Guarantee an inheritance
- Build generational momentum intentionally

It is stable. It is tax-advantaged. It is accessible. And, it is one of the few wealth tools that involves no risk and is not dependent on credit, income brackets, or institutional approval.

The same institution once used to devalue our lives is now the one that elevates our legacy.

Chapter 6: What Are Living Benefits?

To understand life insurance it's important to know its' inner workings. Most people think of life insurance as something that helps only after they've passed on. But, what if the right policy could also protect you while you're alive, when you're sick, recovering, or simply trying to maintain your lifestyle during tough times? Well, these are the things that a policy's living benefits provide… There are many

Living benefits turn your life insurance into a financial lifeline- a source of tax-free funds that can help you and your family survive before you ever need the death benefit. They are the most powerful and overlooked parts of modern life insurance.

Living Benefits- Plain & Simple

Living benefits are features (or "riders"), built into many life insurance policies that allow the owner of the policy to access a portion of the death benefit early, if certain medical conditions or life events happen. There are both paid riders and ones that come standard with certain policies. We're going to talk about the no-cost ones that come standard with the policies we're discussing- Cash Value Accumulation, Terminal, Chronic and Critical Illness riders.

1. Cash Value Accumulation (IUL/Whole Life)

The money for the loan that you have access to is determined by how much is stock piled here. Depending on the type of policy you have, you will accumulate a certain amount of cash on a yearly basis. When you pay your monthly premium, the cost of life insurance will be deducted, and what remains is put into an insurance 'savings' account. Based on the cash value, that account will usually accumulate at a rate of 3%-6% interest on a Whole Life policy, or 0%-Uncapped interest on IUL policies. The time that it takes for the cash to accumulate is a huge factor in determining which policy to use to fund a specific part of a legacy plan.

2. Terminal Illness (Term/IUL/Whole Life)

If you're diagnosed with a terminal illness and a doctor certifies that your life expectancy is typically 12-24 months or less, you can access part of your death benefit right away.

How it helps:

- Pay for care, treatment, or home modifications
- Travel or focus on quality time with loved ones
- Settle affairs while you're still able to make decisions

Example: *If you have a $500,000 policy, you may be able to access $250,000 or more while you're still living, leaving the remainder for your beneficiaries later.*

3. Chronic Illness (Term/IUL)

A chronic illness benefit helps when you can no longer perform everyday tasks without help. If a doctor confirms that you need assistance with at least two Activities of Daily Living (ADLs), like bathing, dressing, eating, or walking, your policy may allow you to access part of your benefit monthly or as a lump sum.

How it helps:

- Pays for in-home care or assisted living
- Covers medical equipment or family caregiving costs
- Maintains dignity and independence without draining savings

Key features to know:

- You can usually take between 2% to 4% of your death benefit per month. For example, if your policy's death benefit is $100,000 and the company allows you 3% per month, that would be $3000 per month to help towards your monthly expenses

- Funds can be used however you choose- not just for medical bills

Example: A $300,000 policy might pay $9,000 per month for up to 33 months if you become chronically ill.

3. Critical Illness (Term/IUL)

Critical illness riders pay out if you experience life-altering medical events- like a heart attack, stroke, cancer diagnosis, or organ transplant.

How it helps:

- Provides fast cash to cover medical bills and lost income
- Prevents you from going into debt or dipping into retirement funds
- Keeps your household afloat during recovery

Common covered conditions include:

- Heart attack
- Stroke
- Major organ transplant
- End-stage renal failure
- Cancer (invasive or late stage)
- Paralysis or severe burns

Example: If you survive a heart attack and your $250,000 policy allows for 50% critical illness access, you could receive $125,000, tax-free, to cover recovery expenses or replace your income.

Final Thoughts

Honestly, I'm really proud of the way you're moving through the material! There's a lot of information and structure to consider. And you're killing it.

Now that you're clear about how living benefits works, in the next chapter, we'll break down **Term, Whole Life, and IULs** and how the varying types of life insurance can work together in, "Understanding the Play".

Chapter 7: Understanding the Play- Wealth Stack Unlocked

(Choosing the Right Type of Life Insurance for Your Legacy Goals)

Mainstream financial education surrounding building wealth focuses heavily on savings accounts, 401(k)s, investments, ROTH IRAs and homeownership (to name a few), which are great options, but all require a level of both risk and loss. However, life insurance- **Term, IUL, Whole Life with Paid-Up Additions** and **Annuities** have not been given their proper due in this conversation, because (as previously stated), they are guaranteed tools for growth without risk. AND- not just small growth. But, they do real numbers that can be used as the bedrock of any solid financial family foundation. You're literally winning from knowing where to put your money!

I want to borrow a question that my life insurance colleague, Drew Jerden always asks, "What would you bet if you knew you couldn't lose?". Would you go hard? Or, go home?

I say, GO HARD- We've learned that life insurance isn't one-size-fits-all contract, and that's a good thing. Just like wealth itself, it comes in different forms, each with its own purpose, strengths, and strategies. To be successful in this space, every family needs at least one leader who's going to take time to learn the rules of this game, then make the moves to get their family (team), to the win. Even if you take some missteps in your process- Get in the game, and stay in it. Consult with your broker, your agent- even ChatGPT. Being the head means being responsible for understanding the rules, creating the play, setting your team up for success and putting the players in position to RUN IT.

As the leader of your team, it's super important to make your life insurance strategy- You need a Wealth Stack to win in this game. What Is a **Wealth Stack** you ask? It's a 3 tier (or more), insurance strategy made up of **Term, IUL and Whole Life with Paid Up Addition**s- a layering of insurance policies that solidify an easy and safe path to your family's financial legacy.

Advantages of a Wealth Stack:

- Once you know the differences between **Term, Whole Life, and Indexed Universal Life (IUL),** you can structure them, set-it-and -forget it with auto-pay, and gain year, after year
- You can safeguard and grow your money easily without having to stress over taking losses

- You're in control- You can include as many life insurance policies as you can afford in your stack
- You can edit the Wealth Stack as your family and circumstances change
- You can use big or small money. It all multiplies
- A little knowledge goes a long way. It really pays off

Purpose & Policy

If you need...	Consider...
Immediate, affordable, big	Term Life
A guaranteed inheritance for your family, steady cash value accumulation, investment	Whole Life w/PUA
Flexible, long-term, high-growth potential with tax-free retirement income, living	IUL
A Wealth Stack	Combine all 3 strategically

Term Life Insurance

(Short-Term Coverage with Living/Death Benefits)

What It Is:

- A policy that covers you for a fixed term of time (10, 20, 25 or 30 years)

- Pays a death benefit only if you die during that time frame
- Generally has no cash value and no investment component. Though, as of late, companies have been offering term policies with living benefits and return of premium options

When It Works Best:

- When covering big-ticket responsibilities like:
  - Mortgage protection (pays off your house when you pass away so that your loved ones can keep your home, or pays the balance of the mortgage down to buy time before they sell)
  - Income replacement in the case of your passing (your family doesn't go broke when you pass away)
  - Children's college tuition (your children's future can still be secured, even though you have passed on)
  - Paying off debt that may pass down to your loved ones
- When you need affordable coverage because the budget is tight:
  - Term policies are the least expensive, because they provide your family with the lowest amount of living benefits
  - They provide the least risk and most return for the life insurance companies, because customers either: 1) Don't die within the term of the policy (so they don't pay out), OR 2) Prematurely fall off of their payments before they die (so the company never has to pay the family)

Pros:

- Inexpensive
- High coverage amounts for low monthly premiums
- Great for early-stage wealth protection, young families and protecting big ticket items for a particular time

Considerations:

- No wealth accumulation
- No living benefits (many times)
- If coverage lapses before you pass away your money is lost

Example:

A 35-year-old single mother buys a $500,000 30-year term policy for $30/month to ensure her daughter can finish college and stay in their home if she passes unexpectedly. If the mother actually passes away, her child (once she is 18, gets $500,000 minus any deductions that her mom may have accumulated from using the living benefits). If the woman lives past age 65, her daughter will receive nothing and no cash value will have accumulated.

Whole Life Insurance

(Permanent Coverage- Guaranteed Protection- Steady Wealth Building)

What It Is:

- A permanent policy that lasts your entire life (usually until age 121)
- Includes a guaranteed death benefit
- Builds cash value over time- slowly and steadily
- Gives fast access to cash value

When It Works Best:

- You want to lock in lifelong protection
- You plan to leave a guaranteed inheritance
- You want to create a private reserve of wealth you can access while living

How It Grows:

- Premiums go into the base policy
- Additional contributions (Paid-Up Additions, or PUAs), must be specially set up by your broker/agent to speed up the cash value growth
- If you get the policy through a mutual company, they pay dividends that you can reinvested back into your cash value to increase your benefits

Pros:

- Guaranteed growth
- Pays dividends
- Allows you to use and reuse your cash value to buy assets
- Loans are available tax-free

- Death benefit is guaranteed regardless of market conditions

Considerations:

- Premiums are higher than term
- Cash value builds slower than an IUL
- Best used for self-banking and investment purposes

Example:

A 45-year-old business owner buys a $250,000 Whole Life policy with PUAs. By age 65, it's built approximately $120,000 in cash value, which will fund his cushy retirement rum bar in Barbados. He will also still leave the full benefit from the policy to his children.

Hidden Advantages of Whole Life with Paid-Up Additions (PUAs)

Many people are discouraged to get Whole Life, when they compare the growth of its cash value to the IUL. However, Whole Life still wins, because qualifying for it is more lenient, growth is consistent and it's readily available for investments and transactions when needed.

1. Guaranteed Cash Value Growth

- Every dollar paid into the policy builds guaranteed cash value, regardless of market conditions

- You'll receive a policy illustration that tells you exactly what you're getting from your coverage. It will also include projections of how your cash value will grow

2. Tax-Free Access with No Market Risk

- You can borrow against the policy tax-free without ever worrying about a stock market crash.
- Great for conservative investors, people whose health won't allow them to get an IUL, or elders with low financial risk tolerance.

3. Dividends (Your Policy's Quiet Bonus Check)

- Many mutual insurance companies pay annual dividends which can:
  - ■ Increase cash value
  - ■ Purchase additional paid-up insurance
  - ■ Be taken as income

4. Strong Legacy Play

- Whole life's death benefit is guaranteed
- It's the most trusted tool for legacy gifting, estate planning, and charitable giving

5. Superior for Collateralization

- Often favored by banks and lenders as loan collateral.
- Builds net-worth and diversifies the financial portfolio

- Especially useful for entrepreneurs looking to borrow without affecting credit or selling assets.

6. Premium Flexibility with PUAs

- You can overfund the policy using PUAs to accelerate cash growth
- This flexibility is key for people with variable income (i.e., creatives, entrepreneurs, small biz owners, etc.)

7. Powerful in Trust Planning

- Whole life is ideal for irrevocable life insurance trusts (ILITs) or generational wealth tools because:
  ■ It's stable
  ■ Predictable
  ■ Easy to structure long-term around estate tax issues

8. It's Your Private Bank

- Fund it- Borrow from it- Don't worry about qualifying or being denied
- No repayment schedule required
- You set your own terms

Indexed Universal Life (IUL)

Flexible Coverage with Market-Linked Growth

What It Is:

- A permanent policy (like Whole Life), but with more flexibility

- Gives the policy owner control over what retirement looks like
- Cash value grows based on the performance of a stock market index (ex: the S&P 500)
- Gains only- The policy never loses money, because your money isn't actually in the market
- Typically has the same low price-point and qualifications as a Term policy. So go for the gusto and get an IUL
- Gives Chronic, Critical and Terminal illness coverage (Living Benefits/disability coverage), after 90 days of illness
- Adds a safety layer to whatever coverage you may already have
- Creates an element of security for entrepreneurs who are responsible for their own benefits

When It Works Best:

- You want a financial safety net as an entrepreneurs/self-employed person
- You need to build a great retirement plan (or add to a retirement plan)
- You want tax breaks
- You're comfortable with some market-linked variability (without risk)
- You want the flexibility to adjust your premiums or coverage, so that you can grow your cash value faster. Or you can decrease your premium temporarily in hard times

How It Grows:

- When the market index goes up, your cash value earns (often capped at 9–12%, with some companies offering NO CAP interest rates)
- You're never at risk of losing your money in the stock market. When the market goes down, you earn nothing, but you also don't lose anything

Pros:
- Potential for higher cash value growth than Whole Life
- Tax-free loans for income in retirement
- Policy is adjustable (great for entrepreneurs or fluctuating income)

Considerations:
- More complex than Whole Life
- Growth isn't guaranteed, although it's highly unlikely to not grow in successive years
- Must be structured properly to avoid overfunding or lapsing

Example:
A 38-year-old teacher opens an IUL with $500/month. After 20 years, they begin pulling $20,000 per year tax-free as supplemental retirement income, all while keeping a death benefit in place.

Final Thoughts

Life insurance is a team sport. As the leader, choosing a life insurance policy isn't just a financial decision, it's a generational one that will effect your bloodline in a future you will never see. Each type of coverage has its place, serving a specific purpose. And, even if you don't get it perfect from the start, you can adjust. It''s not about where you start, but how you finish. You are the head of your squad. Keep guidance and your family's long-term future in mind as you move toward your wins.You're making marathon moves.

In the next chapter, we'll expand on the previous ideas. Let's apply them based on age, budget, and goals, to get to the meat and potatoes of how a Wealth Stack looks.

Chapter 8: Wealth Stack Part I- START NOW

The Wealth Stack is my term for a practical 3 tier insurance system that protects, grows, and passes down wealth. Now that we know that the wealth gap was made by design, it is important to intentionally construct a way out. Though being properly insured is not a fix-all, but it's definitely a strong plan. ***The Wealth Stack*** can be the bridge over troubled waters.

The key to a **Wealth Stack** is to start where you are, and have the patience to work your plan over time. A huge misconception about life insurance is that it's only valuable when a person has a hefty death benefit. Many people want a $1,000,000 policy, but many times they don't really know why or realize how much it costs to maintain it. Nothing could be further from the truth. It's important to tailor your policies to suit your needs. And, it's totally fine to build out multiple policies as your cashflow and

income grows. Remember, life insurance is a long-term game. Where you start doesn't have to be where you finish.
You may want a $100,000 policy, but your current income and health/medical records dictates that you can afford a $25,000 policy right now. It's important to know that as your money and health improve, you can add on more policies. Be clear- $25,000+$25,000+25,000+$25,000, still equals $100,000! The key is accumulating as much as you can, as early as you can. Things like cost of living raises, inheritances, settlements and windfalls of cash are great opportunities to 'insure up', with either all or some of the money.

The Wealth Stack- *Policies Working Together:*
Each family should devise a plan with their insurance that guarantees profits and protection for its' members. It should be made up of at least 3 life insurance policies that pay out to the family's trust (preferably), or to its beneficiaries.
Let's look at some scenarios of how to insure within each age group, a range of monthly payments, and how it all ties together to build a proper **Wealth Stack.**

Remember: All of these are life insurance policy options that still must be qualified for as usual.

Sample Cash Value Scenarios by Age & Policy Type

Disclaimer: The following examples are for illustrative purposes only. Actual results will vary based on the insured's age, health, the insurance company, the premium structure, and the policy performance. These numbers assume a healthy, non-smoking individual, using well-structured policies. Always consult a licensed advisor for a personalized illustration. Again, this is only for illustrative purposes.

Here are some examples of how stacking insurance can work:

Policy Type	Purpose	Role in the Stack
Term	Affordable coverage for major	Protects income, mortgage, college
IUL	Long-term wealth building + retirement	Grows tax-free income you can access, preferably
Whole Life (PUAs)	Guaranteed death benefit + private reserve	Legacy protection + family funding source. investment

Stage 1: Birth to Age 20

(Start Early. Let Time Do the Heavy Lifting)

Strategy:

- Open a **Whole Life** or **IUL** policy for a newborn or child as soon as possible

- The earlier the policy starts, the more time it has to grow cash value
- Over time, this policy can fund first car, college, or even a first home, while still protecting the family and paying for burial

Monthly Recommendation:
- $50–$200/month
- Add **Paid-Up Additions (Whole Life)** to accelerate growth

Why It Works:
- Locks in insurability while they're young and healthy
- Lets compound interest and dividends build over decades
- Pricing stays the same (unless you do add ons at specific times)
- Lasts forever (only cancels for non-payment)

Stage 2: Age 21–35
(Start Protection As You Build Your Foundation)

Strategy:
- Begin with a low-cost **Term** policy that protects your children, covers the income, mortgage and debt lost when you pass away. Get 7-10x your income
- Open your **IUL** and start building for retirement and future cash
- Add a modest **Whole Life with PUAs** policy to build long-term, guaranteed money and extra money for your family

Monthly Recommendation:

- $200–$500/month combined across 2–3 policies
- Be strategic and direct policies toward specific life events, (i.e., mortgage, college, loans)

Why It Works:

- **Term** is affordable and offers peace of mind (approx. $25-$75)
- **IUL** sets up future income beyond your 401(k) (approx. $175-$300)
- **Whole Life** builds steady, liquid wealth over time (approx. $50-$125)

Stage 3: Age 36–50

Stack Intentionally. Protect, Grow, and Position Your Assets.

Strategy:

Increase **Term** coverage if income or family needs have grown

Maximize **IUL** contributions to prepare for early retirement income

Use **Whole Life** policies to fund a trust or leave behind wealth

Monthly Recommendation:

- $500–$1,000/month depending on income, marital status and children

Why It Works:

- **Term Life** (wealth-minded people usually have 7-10 times their yearly income)
- **IUL** (premium = 5-7% of your monthly income. It diversifies your retirement strategy and customizes your future lifestyle while you still have time to compound lots of interest)
- **Whole Life with Paid Up Additions** (premium = 3-7% of your monthly income- Focuses on long-term guaranteed cash value, estate planning and investment capital)
- You're in your highest earning years of your life
- Life insurance gives both protection and control over how your money moves
- It's easier to preserve wealth than rebuild it

Additional Moves:

- Get a trust and include your policies
- Use policy loans for real estate or business investments
- Name contingent beneficiaries for layers of protection

*** **Key Note:** *These percentages are guides- some high net-worth families pour 20-25% of their income into permanent insurance as a wealth strategy*

Bonus Tip:

Consult with a seasoned professional to consider drawing policies on healthy adult children/grandchildren to build wealth more efficiently

Stage 4: Age 51+

(Preserve Wealth and Ensure the Transfer Is Clean)

Strategy:

- If new to insurance: begin with **IUL** (if you can qualify)/ **Whole Life** for long-term guarantees and easy final expense is s great secondary
- If already covered: review policies and layer them in trusts or annuities
- Use life insurance to cover final expenses, estate taxes, or legacy gifts

Monthly Recommendation:

- Varies based on goals and health. Start with a legacy plan and reverse engineer
- If possible, $500–$1,000+/month depending on income and age

Why It Works:

- These are the years of continuing to add funds to your policies- to set up the next generation, to make withdrawals from your policies, for plans that you'd previously. Or, it may be time to start pulling loans from your policies (depending on your plan)

- You can set up policies for grandchildren, build Trusts (with your lawyers), with roles assigned to your family members, and further create wealth for future generations

Bonus Tip:

- Use your remaining years to shift from earning money to collecting, directing and distributing monies with your broker, lawyer and good old AI

*** ***Reach out to www.YvetteBMotivates.com for more information on how to strategize and create your Wealth Stack.***

Chapter 9: The Wealth Stack Part II- MORE

(Insure. Invest. Inherit.)

Cover What Matters Now

TIER 1: INSURE

Foundation- basic coverage to protect your income, loved ones, and obligations.

Primary Tool: Term Life Insurance

- Affordable, high-coverage protection for 10–30 years
- Replaces your income if you pass away early
- Covers major expenses like:
  - Mortgage
  - Children's education
  - Final expenses
  - Bills/loans

Strategy:

- Start with a term policy that is 7-10x your annual income.

- You can stack policies of various value, if you getting a large amount at one time is challenging

Example:

- 30-year-old with $70k income = $490,000–$700,000 term policy
- $30–$70/month (qualification depends on your health)

Low-cost, immediate coverage examples:

Start Age	Monthly Cost	Coverage Term	Death Benefit
25	$25/mo	30 years	$300,000
35	$35/mo	30 years	$500,000
45	$65/mo	30 years	$450,000

Pure protection- No cash value

Why this matters:

Protects your family from financial devastation while you build wealth.

- Affordable, immediate, high-coverage protection for 10–30 years
- Ideal for covering mortgage, children's security, college, spousal support or income that would be missing when you pass away

- Some term policies offer living benefits and/or a return of all (or some), of the premiums you pay over the years (Ask your broker or agent to tell you more)

TIER 2: INVEST
Grow Money While You're Here (aka- Living Benefits)

This is where you kickstart your wealth- the part of your plan that builds cash value over time and gives you access to money while you're living.

Primary Tool: Indexed Universal Life (IUL)
- Stock Market-linked cash growth (0% floor- NO Cap)
- Optional increasing death benefit
- Tax-deferred cash accumulation
- Tax-free policy loans for:
  - ■ Retirement income
  - ■ Business investment
  - ■ Real estate down payments
  - ■ Emergency funds

Strategy:
- Overfund your IUL up to the IRS limits (avoid Modified Endowment Contract, MEC status), to maximize growth.
- The best results come from letting cash value grow for 10-15 years before accessing it to improve profitability

Example:

- A healthy 35-year-old contributes $300/month
- By retirement, they can access $25k+/year tax-free for 15+ years

Indexed Universal Life (IUL)

Chart shows market-linked growth (0% floor, 9% cap)

Start Age	Monthly Contribution	Projected Cash Value	Potential Tax-Free Income
25	$100/mo	~$41,000 (20 yrs)	~$10,000/year for 10 years (starting ~65)
35	$300/mo	~$115,000 (20 yrs)	~$25,000/year for 15 years (starting ~65)
45	$500/mo	~$152,000 (20 yrs)	~$27,000/year for 15 years (starting ~70)

RECAP: *Market-linked growth (0% floor, 9% cap) with tax-free loan potential. I know I'm repeating, but I want to make it very plain. Examples are purely standard level calculations for visuals. Illustrated at 7%*

- Female Age 25 – $100/mo:
  Cash Value at 20 yrs: approx. $41,000 with $100,000 death benefit
  Tax-Free Income at 65: approx. $20000/yr for 10 yrs

- Male Age 35 – $300/mo:
  Cash Value at 20 yrs: approx. $115,000 with $300,000 death benefit
  Tax-Free Income at 65: approx. $18000/yr for 15 yrs
- Male Age 45 – $500/mo:
  Cash Value at 20 yrs: ~$175000 with $300,000 death benefit
  Tax-Free Income at 70: ~$18,000/yr for 15 yrs

Why this matters:

Builds wealth very much like 401(k)s and IRAs with liquidity and fewer restrictions.

- IULs give you the power to build your own 401(k)-like savings plan on your own terms. You decide how much you want to contribute each month to get the financial outcome you want by a certain age
- The monthly payments are flexible. You can also pay a little extra without getting into tax trouble. If you find yourself in a bind, you can pay a bit less. All of these numbers will be specified in your policy illustration
- You only experience the gains of the stock market without any losses
- It's one of the safest and most lucrative financial plays to have in your fiscal playbook
- Popular among entrepreneurs and retirement planners
- Must be designed properly to avoid lapses or tax penalties

TIER 3: INHERIT

Strategy:

Preserve & Transfer Wealth the Right Way

This is your *legacy layer*, structured to pass down money TAX & DRAMA-FREE

Primary Tool: Whole Life Insurance with Paid-Up Additions (PUAs)

- Guaranteed cash value + death benefit
- Tax-free inheritance
- Optional dividends (from mutual companies- definitely SAY YES when you have this option!)
- Can be owned by a **TRUST** for legal protection and estate planning

Strategy:

Use Whole Life to:

- Leave behind exactly how much cash you want
- Construct/Fund your family trust
- Cash and death benefits can't be lost in probate or court
- Also a great option if you're not sure you want to be a homeowner. Gives excellent returns without the extra responsibilities attached

Example:

- 45-year-old puts $1,000/month into a Whole Life policy for 20 years

Builds approx. $180k+ in cash value
Leaves approx. $500,000+ between cash value and death benefit to their family through their trust

Whole Life Insurance with Paid-Up Additions (PUAs)
Steady, guaranteed growth + potential dividends

RECAP: *Steady, guaranteed growth + potential dividends*

When it comes to your children. Get insurance for them as soon as they pop out! Here's a simple play that you can use, with whatever amount of money you can afford.

- From birth to Age 18:
  - ■ Open a Whole Life policy or Indexed Universal Life (IUL) as early as possible
  - ■ Add Paid-Up Additions (PUAs) or overfund the policy to grow long-term value
  - ■ Protect your children and grandchildren early while building a wealth tool they can access later
- Male Age 0 (Child): approx. $50/mo:
  Cash Value at 18: approx. $7500 with $97,000 death benefit
  Cash Value at 40: approx. $3000
- Female Age 15: $100/mo:
  Cash Value at 20 yrs: approx. $26,000 with $250,000 death

benefit
Cash Value at 40 yrs: approx. $160,000

- Female Age 45 – $300/mo:
  Cash Value at 20 yrs: approx. $69,000
  Cash Value at 30 yrs: approx. $122,000

Why Whole Life with PUA's matter:

- Very safe
- Ideal for building a slow, guaranteed reserve of wealth
- Great place to hold lump sums of money that allows instant access and the ability to earn interest

Yields great returns when you dump a lump sum into the policy, plus pay a monthly premium

Chapter 10: How to Borrow From Your Policy

Now that you're familiar with the benefits of having the various types of policies, it's important to know how to access money when you need it. Always take into consideration that each company has its' own set of procedures, so steps for some companies will differ from others. Let's go over a few points to get familiar with the borrowing process.

Borrowing from an IUL:

The First Step: Call A Professional

Although this step is very important, it's surprising that many people don't consider reaching out to their insurance broker or agent to assist them before taking money from their policy. Borrowing from your life insurance isn't super complicated, but it helps to talk things out to be clear about your goals and strategies.

Points to consider:

1- Only borrowing from your policy to purchase assets
2- Buying things that are instrumental to advancing you and your family's future
3- Having a self-governed repayment plan in place before you borrow the money

2. Check Your Cash Value

Your next move is to grab a copy of your policy with the illustration inside, which gives you all of the details of your contract. It also has a Tabular Detail or Numeric Summary that explains the projected amount of cash value that is available for you to borrow.

Login to the company's portal to check your policy's exact cash value. The amount is based on accumulated cash value minus any surrender charges or outstanding loans plus interest. Then, call your insurance carrier to confirm the numbers and get your loan started.

It's wise to take a **loan** or **participating loan** (if possible), when accessing your money. It's NOT recommended to **withdraw** from your policy, because it often leads to tax implications. And nobody wants to talk to the IRS! With a loan, your interest rate will be a bit higher, but it pays off in the end.

**Side note: It's never advisable to borrow more than 90% of your cash value, if you want your policy to remain in effect.*

3. Request the IUL loan

Taking a Participating Loan on an IUL is very beneficial. It allows you to earn interest on your cash value, even when you've subtracted from it. No credit checks or hassles. You simply request the amount you need, and the insurance company either mails you a check or direct deposits directly into your bank (usually in 48 to 72 hours).

Loan accrues interest

Low interest on the loan (typically between 4-8% annually).

- Participating loan: When you borrow, your cash value still earns index credits.
- Standard IUL loan: When borrowing at a fixed 5-6%, from an IUL, cash value is not earning index credits (makes your money works harder to earn)

Pros and Cons of borrowing from your IUL

Pros

- No credit checks (you're borrowing from yourself)
- Flexible repayment schedule (you decide when/how to repay yourself)
- Tax-advantaged: loan proceeds are generally not taxable

Cons

- If unpaid, the loan + interest reduces your death benefit

- If the loan balance grows too large, the policy can lapse (triggering taxes. Never exceed 90% of your cash value)
- Don't risk policy lapse- Interest accrues-

Example: Borrowing & Paying Yourself Back-
Imagine you've built $50,000 in cash value

- You borrow $20,000 at 5% interest
- Annual loan interest = about $1,000 (5% of $20,000)
- Your un-borrowed $30,000 will still be earning 5–7% index growth in a good year

4. Repayment Strategy
Instead of just "paying money back," this is your opportunity to turn repayment into a wealth cycle:

- Use the $20,000 to invest in something income-producing (e.g., buy a vending machine route, invest in a dividend stock portfolio, or fund a small business project)
- Let's say that investment makes you $500/month
- You commit $400/month to repay your policy loan and keep $100/month as profit- WINNING!

After about 4–5 years, the loan is fully repaid. Your IUL cash value is restored (and still growing), plus you created an outside income stream.

Simple Repayment "Hack"

Treat your IUL loan like your own bank:

- **Step 1**: Set a monthly autopay (e.g., $400).
- **Step 2:** Always pay back principal + interest, just as if it were a bank loan.
- **Step 3:** Redirect any extra cash flow from investments/ businesses into your policy to grow it even faster.

Borrowing from a Whole Life with Paid Up Additions (PUA):

** Both Whole Life and IUL loans involve using your cash value as collateral. Growth, risks, costs, and controls are very different.*

How Whole Life loans are different:

A **Whole Life** contract has a **Base Policy**: The guaranteed core amount of your death benefit and cash value that your initial premium payment bought. It's guaranteed by the insurance carrier. The cash value grows modestly over time.

Paid-Up Additions: Mini life policies added to the contract to increase the policy's death benefit and cash value. You can buy them using extra premium generated by your earned dividends. Once you pay the initial amount, no future premiums are needed. The additions gain cash value just like the base policy does. These paid additions are made up of **Non-Direct**

Recognition (NDR) or **Direct Recognition** (DR), depending on the company you choose.

Ultimately, Base + PUA's = your total super charged cash value pool

1. **Reach out to your broker/agent**
2. **Check availability of funds-** log in or call your carrier to confirm:
3. **Request the loan- no credit check-** the policy is the collateral and choose disbursement (ACH to your bank or a check by mail)
4. **Keep the policy healthy**
   - Keep premiums paid
   - Check in with your broker at least once a year
   - Pay loan interest from outside funds (don't let it roll into the loan if you can help it)
   - Continue PUA contributions to keep your interest compounding strongly
   - Review the annual illustration/statement to ensure loan + interest isn't overtaking growth of cash value
5. **Know whether your insurance company offers Dividend, Recognition** (DR)**, or Non-Direct Recognition** (NDR), **as its dividend payment scale.**
6. **With NDR, your entire cash value keeps compounding as if you hadn't borrowed any of it, even when you have-** The insurance company does not change how it credits dividends on your cash value, even if some is loaned out. This loan type is popular because your entire cash value

keeps earning the same dividend rate, whether you've borrowed or not. It allows you to basically break even when you borrow.

7. DR reduces dividend on the borrowed portion- Net borrowing costs feel higher. The insurance company adjusts the dividend on the portion of your cash value that's being used as collateral for a loan. You still get dividends, but they're different on the loaned portion vs. the unloaned portion.

Pros

- No credit check; fast access to liquidity.
- Flexible repayment (you choose timing/amount).
- PUAs turbocharge CV, so your borrowing power can rebuild quickly if you keep funding.

Cons

- If you don't pay interest, the balance can snowball and threaten lapse of policy
- Dividends are not guaranteed; loan rate may be fixed or variable and can change
- **Modified Endowment Contract** (MEC), risk if you overfund PUA's too aggressively; MEC is the implication that you're using the policy as an investment to hide your money rather than a life insurance policy- with benefits. That has tax consequences.

Example Borrowing & Paying Yourself Back:

Beginning Cash value = \$100,000

- Borrow = \$40,000
- Dividend rate = 5%
- Company credits 5% on the entire \$100,000 = \$5,000 dividend
- Loan interest (say 5%) accrues separately on the \$40,000 loan = \$2000

You're up \$3000

Direct Recognition (DR) option: The insurance company adjusts the dividend on the portion of your cash value that's being used as collateral for a loan. You still get dividends, but they're different on the loaned portion vs. the (un)loaned portion.

Example:

- Cash value = \$100,000
- Borrow = \$40,000
- Dividend rate on (un)borrowed \$60,000 = 5% → \$3,000
- Dividend rate on borrowed \$40,000 might be lowered to 2% → \$800
- Total dividend = \$3,800 instead of \$5,000

Dividends are not guaranteed and depend on the carrier. The recognition method determines how dividends are credited when you have a loan outstanding.

Repayment Strategy

Scenario (example to make it easy):

- Cash value: $100,000 (base + PUAs)
- Borrow: $40,000
- Loan rate: 5% → interest ≈ $2,000/year initially
- Recognition: NDR (your entire CV still participates in dividends)

The plan

1. **Keep interest current (non-negotiable).**
2. **Set a principal schedule you'll actually keep.**
3. **Rebuild while you repay.**
    - Add conservatively each month to PUAs (stay under MEC).
    - This keeps your cash value compounding and replenishes the borrowing capacity

Result: In 5 years, loan is gone, interest never capitalized, and your PUA-fueled cash value is larger than before. After payoff, keep sending the same monthly amount to PUAs for 12–24 months to "overfill your tank." You can repeat this process for as many times as your budget allows. You can either get more policies with the same company, up to their insurance cap amount. Or, you can repeat the process with as many companies as you can afford.

4. Rinse & Repeat

Final Thoughts

You don't need to wait to become millionaires or billionaires before you start using the strategies the wealthy have used since insurance was invented. Move intentionality, with education, and consistency. What the Rockefellers did with millions, you can also do by starting right from wherever you are. You can build your own empire from the ground up.

Chapter 11: FIXED INDEX ANNUITIES

(Making Your Money Work Beyond the Bank)

Savings accounts are funny. You 'safely' hold your money in the bank and earn 1- 4% interest off loaning your hard earned cash to the institution of your choice. The bank invests those cash holdings (from its customers), into mostly life insurance and real estate, making a huge profit- They then loan the money back to their customer at an elevated rate, and make a killing. Ironically, this is known to the customer as SAVINGS. Stay with me- we're going to land on **Fixed Index Annuities.**

Ultimately, keeping large sums of money in a traditional savings account is a losing game for the consumer. It's like having a Ferrari that you lend to a friend to go out on the town. You're generous enough to let them ride nice and shine, while *you* pay the cost to be a boss!

This Brings Us To Fixed Index Annuities-

At its' core, a **Fixed Index Annuity** (FIA), is also a form of savings account- It's a long-term, tax-deferred savings contract (policy), with a life insurance company that takes at least $10,000 to start. It earns high yielding interest (usually between 5- 11%), and can be held for a time period of 5, 7, 10 or 14 years, depending on the company.

The FIAs best feature is that, after the time has ended, the owner of the policy can begin receiving payments back from the money and interest accumulated. Those payments will keep coming until the policy owner passes away, if the owner hasn't opted to take it in a lump sum.

Because the FIA has a protective floor of 0%, just like an IUL or Whole Life policy, there is never any risk of losing the money that's being accumulated. The guaranteed minimum interest rate insures that the annuity still gains even when the market performs poorly. This provides a reliable paycheck in retirement years. (There are various types of annuities. We're focusing only on **Fixed Index Annuities**, because most insurance brokers and agents are qualified to offer them to customers).

A Few Reasons To Get An FIA:

- You want a safe place to sit your money where it can collect guaranteed interest for a specific timeframe
- You're past the age of getting a traditional life insurance policy

- You can't qualify for coverage due to poor health and have money sitting in savings
- You're under 5,7,10 or 14 years from being 59 1/2 years old and want to set up your own early pension.
- You want to lessen the chances of your money taking a hit from inflation
- You want tax deferred growth

Why Not Just Use a Savings Account?
In theory, a savings accounts feel safe. You can open your bank app, look at your money and know that it's all there- snug as a bug in a rug. You can get to it whenever you need it. But here's the hidden danger that's putting your comfy cozy money at risk: **INFLATION.**

Considerations-
- Average savings account interest = .01% to .046%
- So: $100,000 sitting in a savings account will receive between $1000-$4600 in interest for the year
- Average inflation = .02% to .045% per year (and higher in recent years)
- Which takes $2000- $4500 off of the value of the $100,000 per year
- The average FIA pays between .05% to .11% on your $100,000

Which adds $5000- $11000 to the FIA and makes up the

losses from inflation

You don't have to be a genius to know that bank math is risky! Every year that your money is sitting in savings it could quietly be losing buying power. On average, if you can afford to let your money sit, an FIA is a far better value than going with the bank.

How To Buy & Set Up a Fixed Index Annuity

When setting up your FIA, make sure to have a reputable life insurance broker that represents A-rated companies to assist you with your process. Prepare to be patient. The process can take anywhere from 1 week to 5 months, depending on how you are funding the annuity.

- Select a trustworthy broker to submit your suitability criteria and application
- Choose your timeframe and the index strategy that works best for you
- Choose optional riders, if desired
- Name your beneficiary
- Deposit your payment of $10,000-$2,000,000 into the annuity
- Keep your FIA records with your important documents
- Watch your money grow

The insurance company should provide regular communications via their portal or statements (at least annually), showing you your account value.

How To Withdraw From a Fixed Index Annuity

When you're ready to withdraw funds in retirement, contact your broker. He or she will help you to connect with your insurance company. Most contracts (but not all), will allow a lump-sum withdrawal or annuitization options (either payments that last for a 10 or 20 year fixed term, or lifetime payments).

Be mindful: You can withdraw money from these annuities before age 59 ½, but it's not always a good idea, because you're still young enough to pay high taxes. Many times people under 59 1/2 will roll their money into another annuity after their timeframe has ended to make the most of the tax breaks. Early withdrawals will get in your pockets with interest and fees. You may have to pay regular income tax, a federal tax penalty, and a withdrawal charge. Sometimes you can qualify for a waiver if you meet certain criteria, i.e., entering a nursing facility, developing a terminal illness, or losing your unemployment benefits. Otherwise one must be savvy in strategizing how to maximize the opportunity.

FIA Pros:

- **Earns guaranteed interest:** Like a supercharged Certificate of Deposit (CD)
- **Safety of principal:** The money you pay to purchase the annuity, and the risk-free gains are paid out to you in full or over your lifespan, are never at risk of loss

- **Growth:** Interest rates beat savings accounts
- **Hedge Against Inflation:** FIAs help your savings outpace the loss from inflation
- **Lifetime income options:** You have the power to create your own pension. You put money in, let it grow for a specific time, collect your payments or roll it back into another annuity
- **Pass value to your beneficiaries:** When you pass away, your family gets your annuity balance
- **Yearly withdrawal allowance:** Most companies allow a 10% penalty-free withdrawal every year
- **Age acceptability:** If you've passed the age or health of insurability, or you're close to retirement age it's a solid option for growth on your money

FIA Cons:

- **Money is less liquid:** FIAs are not liquid- They are designed as long-term savings plans. Withdrawals may have penalties in early years. If you need to withdraw funds before the end of the surrender period you will face hefty charges
- **Returns are usually lower than aggressive stock market investing:** Your FIA returns will not exceed the interest cap that is in place no matter how much the stock market gains
- **Taxes on earnings:** When you eventually take withdrawals, the gains are taxed as ordinary income (take your age into consideration for tax breaks)

- **Annual Fees:** Some annuities have ongoing annual fees, which can reduce your overall return
- **Riders:** Adding optional riders for benefits like long-term care can further reduce your contract's value and returns

Final Thoughts

Annuities aren't perfect for everyone. But for people who want safety, interest rates that exceed the banks, and income they can't outlive, they are one of the most powerful tools available. Keeping your money in a savings account might feel secure, but in reality it's a slow leak. Inflation is eroding your wealth every single day. With an annuity you're putting gas in that Ferrari! You're protecting your principal while giving your money a chance to ease on down the road.

Key Lesson: Don't let your hard-earned dollars sit idle. Grow the money- Preserve the money- And protect the money!

CHAPTER 12: Activating Wealth

(Having life insurance is one thing. Using it as part of your family's playbook is next level)

Easy Activation

Though the process may seem scary, taking daily steps towards a life changing family legacy isn't very hard at all. Sometimes the most difficult thing is the internal conflict of knowing where you see your family in the future, but not having a roadmap to get there. That's why, *'Cultivate Legacy'* was created- to be a shortcut on that path to your family's riches.

Step 1: Choose Your Team

You can't run a play without teammates.

- Find a licensed life insurance broker to put the policies in place that best fit your budget and lifestyle
- Pick your people (beneficiaries, trustees, guardians)
- (Bonus): Find an Estate Attorney who do does wills & trusts

Step 2: Get the Right Policy

Think of your policy as your family's emergency parachute + investment plan.

- Use **Term** Insurance for big-ticket needs like protecting, spouse, children, mortgage and funeral expenses
- Use an **IUL** for the same uses as a **Term** AND/OR for building retirement or future wealth while you're alive
- Use **Whole Life** for steady growth, a simple death benefit and for leveraging when it's time to make investments

Start where you are. Begin as early and young as possible. Even $25–$100 a month makes a difference over time.

Step 3: Set It and Schedule It

Money loves a plan. Life loves a calendar.

- Auto-draft your premium payments
- Create a yearly insurance review
- Schedule yearly "family legacy dinner" and talk about your family's future financial vision

Step 4: Use the Policy While You're Alive

This is not "just in case I die" money. It's "so I can live" money.

- Borrow cash from **IUL** or **Whole Life** to invest in assets that pay you back, so that you can re-power up your policy's cash value and repeat the process again, and again

- Supplement your retirement income tax-free

Step 5: Teach Your Family the Playbook

If you don't pass the ball, the team can't win.

- Teach your family about what you've set up
- Explain where the policy is and how it works
- Talk to your heirs about your family's vision

Final Thoughts

Make sure that you, your children, your grandchildren, your immediate family members and your friends know how insurance works and starts exactly where they are to create their wealth journey, *NOW.*

Chapter 13: Questions to Ask Your Agent

(Closed mouths don't build empires)

The 11 Do-or-Die Questions That Protect Your Legacy

Here are 11 must-ask questions that open the door to clarity, protection, and power. They can make or break your financial future. Be sure to bring this list to every meeting:

1. How will this policy best serve my family?
Ask details about how the policy and payout works and how it aligns with your family's needs.

2. Does the policy gain cash value?
Understand if and how your money grows over time. Ask when that growth begins and how it compounds. Also, get an illustration when relevant

3. Is the price locked in?

Clarify whether your monthly premium stays the same or increases over time. A great company's prices are locked in

4. What happens if I miss a payment?
Ask about grace periods, reinstatement rules, and how the policy lapse is set.

5. Will me and my family have access to you if we have questions or need help?
You need to know how to contact your agent and who will help your family file a claim or if you have questions. If something ever happens to you, your family knows who to call first.

6. Are there riders or add-ons I should consider- like Critical Illness or Long-term Care?
Optional riders can give added protection and flexibility. Ask what's included and what's extra.

7. What's the interest rate or dividend rate, and is it guaranteed?
Whole life pays dividends. IULs track market indexes. Know what's fixed and what's variable.

8. How do I maximize my benefits and cash value?
Ask how to structure your policy to build wealth and access it while you're living.

9. Can you help me to build my wealth strategy for my family and future generations?
A strong agent will show you how life insurance fits into a legacy-building game plan.

10. Can you please give me a receipt for the transactions that we've done today?
Always get proof of payment and documentation of your policy details.

11. If you had a choice, would you buy this policy? Why?
This is the real test. See if they stand by what they're recommending. If there's hesitation, you're with the wrong agent/broker.

Bonus Question:* **Who is the key player in taking care of you and your family's needs?
The honest answer is: YOU

The plans, protections, and people you put in place today will make all the difference in the success of your family's future.

Key Players & Plays

1. Your Life Insurance Agent or Broker

They help your family:

- Design policies that specifically meet the needs of each member
- Understand how to use cash value and funds strategically
- Access policy benefits by being the liaison to the company
- File the death claims

Make sure that you have your agent's name, phone, and email in a clearly labeled place on, or with each family member's policy.

2. A Trustworthy Beneficiary, Executor or Trustee

This person will:

- Executor: Carries out your wishes (especially if you've set up a will or living trust), and disperses belongings
- Beneficiary: Receives the death benefit (cash pay out), from your life insurance policy. Pays for your final expenses and distributes monies under the direction of your will or living trust
- Executor/Beneficiary/Trustee: Distribute assets to your family according to your instructions

Choose someone responsible, emotionally stable, and preferably not too overwhelmed with their own affairs.

Be sure to create a will or living trust (with the help of an attorney if possible), to give instructions on how to disperse your legacy.

3. An Estate Planning Attorney (or Pre-Written Legal Docs)

They make sure:

- Your assets are distributed the way your want
- Your family members understand the terms of your legal documents
- Your estate avoids probate (or moves through it smoothly), and stays within the confines of the law
- Minor children are cared for by the right people
- Debts are settled correctly

If you don't have an attorney, use online platforms like Trust & Will or FreeWill to create a basic plan and have it notarized. As soon as possible is always best. Getting an attorney is optimal. Sometimes we don't have as much time as we think.

4. Your Playbook: A Legacy Binder or Digital Vault

- Create a binder or digital folder with:
- Policy numbers & contact info
- Bank account details
- Will/trust documents
- Cell phone/email/computer passcodes
- Instructions for your final wishes (funeral, memorial, etc.)
- A personal letter to your loved ones (optional but deeply meaningful)

5. You- Through the Systems You Set Up Now

You can make it easier, gentler, and even empowering for your family when they need help most.

How?

- Fund your policy consistently
- Keep the beneficiaries of your policies updated
- Review your plan yearly
- Have real conversations with your team now (while you're well)
- Talk to your family about the importance and function of life insurance. Send them this book or schedule a group presentation

Final Thoughts

There are no dumb questions when it comes down to protecting your interests. You're buying life insurance, you're not just getting a policy- You're making life changing decisions about the wealth and lifestyle of your future generations. Too many people sign on the dotted line without asking the right questions. But not you- You will not make the mistakes of the uninformed.

Chapter 14:

WORKBOOK PAGES

Design Your Dynasty: A Wealth Legacy Workbook

(*A Finance, Fashion & Fly SH*T* Companion Tool)

This workbook is your family's legacy blueprint. It helps organize your life insurance, beneficiaries, wealth strategies, and final wishes. It is designed to grow as your assets grow.

1. My Legacy Vision

What do I want life insurance to do for my family?

____

____

____

____

____

What legacy do I want to leave financially, emotionally and spiritually?

____

____

____

____

____

____

2. My Life Insurance Policies

(You can list multiple — this workbook allows space for at least four)

Term Life Policy

- Carrier/Company: ______________________
- Policy #: ______________________
- Death Benefit ($): ______________________
- Start Date: ______________________
- Term Length: ______________________
- Monthly Premium ($): ______________________
- Purpose: ______________________
- Agent Name + Contact: ______________________
- Loan Access (if any): ______________________

Indexed Universal Life (IUL) Policy

- Carrier/Company: ____________________________
- Policy #: ____________________________
- Death Benefit ($): ____________________________
- Cash Value ($): ____________________________
- Start Date: ____________________________
- Monthly Premium ($): ____________________________
- Index Strategy: ____________________________
- Loan Access Instructions: ____________________________
- Agent Name + Contact Info:

  ____
- Purpose: ____

Whole Life with Paid-Up Additions (PUA)

- Carrier/Company: ____________________________
- Policy #: ____________________________
- Death Benefit ($): ____________________________
- Dividend Strategy: ____________________________
- Start Date: ____________________________
- Monthly Premium ($): ____________________________
- Cash Value ($): ____________________________
- Loan Access: ____________________________
- Agent Name + Contact Info:

  ____
- Purpose: ____

Other Policies or Riders

- Type: ______________________________
- Carrier: ______________________________
- Coverage Amount: ______________________________
- Special Notes: ______________________________
- Type: ______________________________
- Carrier: ______________________________
- Coverage Amount: ______________________________
- Special Notes: ______________________________
-
- Type: ______________________________
- Carrier: ______________________________
- Coverage Amount: ______________________________
- Special Notes: ______________________________

3. My Beneficiaries

(Room for at least 10 entries)

4. Bank + Investment Accounts

(Crypto, business, real estate, and checking/savings accounts)

5. Legal + Estate Team

- Executor/Trustee:

  ____

- Estate Attorney (Firm + Contact):

  ____

- Location of Will or Trust Docs:

____

- Guardianship Plan (If applicable):

____

6. Monthly Wealth Commitments

Track your consistent contributions toward the Black Wealth Stack

7. Final Wishes

Preferred Funeral Home:

____

Burial or Cremation:

____

- Special Instructions:

____

____

____

- Spiritual or Cultural Practices:

____

____

____

8. Emergency Action Plan

- Location of password manager or digital vault:

____

Final notes or messages for your family:

Chapter 15: Black Families Need Trusts

A **trust** is a legal tool that allows you to place your assets — such as your home, bank accounts, investments, and life insurance — into a protected structure that is managed according to your explicit instructions.

A trust holds and manages your assets on behalf of your beneficiaries, both while you're alive and after you're gone. It ensures your wishes are followed exactly as you planned. The trust becomes the new "owner" of your assets, and a trusted person (the **trustee**) carries out your wishes for the benefit of the people you choose (your **beneficiaries**). It is one of the most effective ways to protect your wealth, maintain control over how it is used, and ensure that future generations benefit from what you've built.

Why a Trust Matters for Black Families

Unlike a will, a trust:

- **Avoids Probate:** Keeps your family out of expensive, time-consuming court battles
- **Maintains Privacy:** Unlike a will, a trust isn't public records. No one needs to know your business
- **Smooth Transition:** allows your assets to transfer immediately and smoothly
- **Protects Property:** Prevents generational homes and land from being lost or sold off
- **Prepares for Disability:** Your trust can manage your affairs if you become ill or unable to
- **Minimizes Taxes:** Smart trust planning helps preserve more wealth for your heirs
- **Keeps Assets in the Family:** Ensures property, life insurance proceeds, and investments stay under your family's control- not the state's

Example:

If your home and life insurance are owned by your trust, your family won't have to wait months or years for the court to release funds. Everything transfers smoothly, privately, and immediately.

Common Types of Trusts

Not all trusts are the same- and knowing your options helps you choose what fits your goals and budget.

- **Revocable Living Trust:** You control the trust during your lifetime, and it can be changed or canceled at any time. Great for flexibility.
- **Irrevocable Trust**: Once created, it can't be easily changed- but it offers stronger protection from taxes, lawsuits, and creditors.
- **Testamentary Trust:** Created through your will, it activates after your passing. Simple but still requires probate.
- **Special Needs Trust:** Protects loved ones with disabilities without affecting their eligibility for public benefits.
- **Life Insurance Trust (ILIT):** Holds your policy so the death benefit bypasses taxes and goes directly to your heirs.

How to Get a Trust (Even on a Small Budget)
You don't need millions- you just need a plan.

Here are steps you can take today:

1. **List Your Assets:**
   Homes, land, vehicles, businesses, investments, bank accounts, insurance policies- everything that holds value.

2. **Choose Your Beneficiaries:**
   Decide who receives what and how (e.g., age-based disbursements for children or grandkids).

3. **Pick a Trustee:**
   Someone you deeply trust to carry out your wishes responsibly. This could be a family member, friend, or a professional fiduciary.

4. **Consult a Trust Attorney or Service:**

- Traditional attorneys often charge $1,000- $3,000 for a full trust package.
- Affordable alternatives include reputable online services like:
  ■ **Trust & Will**
  ■ **LegalZoom**
  ■ **Nolo**
  ■ **FreeWill** (for simple setups or starting points)
  These platforms offer guided steps and attorney-reviewed documents for a fraction of the cost.

5. **Fund Your Trust:**

Transfer ownership of your assets into the trust- title your property, bank accounts, or policies in its name. (A trust that's not funded is just a piece of paper)

6. **Review & Update Regularly:**

Revisit your trust every 2- 3 years, or after major life changes- births, deaths, marriages, or new properties.

How Funding Your Trust Works

(And Why It's the Most Important Step)

Creating a trust is powerful- but **a trust that isn't funded is an empty shell.**
It's the *funding* that activates the protection, the privacy, and the generational wealth transfer you're building.

To **fund a trust** means to **move assets into** it or legally assign assets so the trust becomes their owner or beneficiary.
Once assets are placed inside the trust, they fall under the trust's rules- *your* rules- and are protected, managed, and distributed the way **you** designed.

Why Funding Your Trust Matters

A trust only works when the things you own are actually placed inside it.
If you don't fund your trust:

- Your assets may still go through probate court
- The state may decide who gets what
- Your heirs may face delays, fees, and conflict
- Your intentions may not be honored
- Creditors may have access to what you meant to protect

Funding the trust ensures:
Immediate transfer of assets without court involvement

- Privacy (your estate is no one's business)
- Control over how, when, and to whom money is released

- Protection for young heirs, blended families, or vulnerable relatives
- Security for your home, accounts, and life insurance

What Assets Can Be Placed in a Trust?

Most people are surprised by how much they can actually place inside a trust.

You can fund a trust with:

- Your home or rental property
- Bank accounts
- Brokerage accounts
- Life insurance policies
- Vehicles (depending on your state)
- Business interests
- Jewelry, art, collectibles
- Retirement accounts (via beneficiary designations)
- Cash reserves
- Future proceeds (like insurance payouts)

How to Fund Your Trust (Step-by-Step)

1. Transfer Ownership of Your Home

Your attorney will help you file a new deed that places the property in the trust's name.

You still control and live in your home. But legally, the trust is the owner.

2. Update Life Insurance Beneficiaries

This is one of the easiest and most powerful steps.

Set your trust as the beneficiary of your:

- Whole Life policies
- IUL policies
- Term policies

When you pass, the death benefit goes directly to the trust (tax-free), and is distributed according to your instructions.

3. Move Bank + Investment Accounts into the Trust

You can either:

- Retitle the accounts in the name of the trust, or
- List the trust as the beneficiary (POD/TOD designation)

Both achieve the goal of bypassing probate.

4. Assign Personal Property to the Trust

Most states allow a simple document within your trust called an Assignment of Personal Property, which transfers:

- Furniture
- Jewelry
- Art
- Family heirlooms
- Business equipment

5. Add Your Business or LLC

If you own a business:

- Add your trust as the owner or primary member
- Update operating agreements and transfer your membership units

This ensures your business doesn't fall apart when you're gone.

6. Confirm Every Asset Has Been Transferred

Your attorney will provide a checklist, but YOU must follow through.

This is one of the most common reasons Black families lose wealth:

the trust is created… but never funded.

Funding a Trust on a Small Budget

You don't need a $5,000 attorney bill to start. Here are practical, legal, budget-friendly options:

Option 1: Online Legal Platforms ($150–$500)

Services like:

- Trust & Will
- Nolo
- LegalZoom

These allow you to create a valid revocable living trust and walk you through funding steps.

Option 2: Low-Cost Estate Clinics

Many cities have:

- University law clinics
- Elder law programs
- Nonprofit legal centers

  that create simple trusts for very low cost or sliding scale.

Option 3: Start with a "Pour-Over Will" + Trust Combo

This protects you even if you haven't transferred everything yet. Anything outside your trust "pours over" into it upon your passing.

Option 4: Start Small + Add Assets Over Time

You don't need everything funded on day one.
Funding can happen in phases:

- Put your life insurance in the trust first
- Add your home next
- Then add accounts as they grow

Trust building is wealth building — and wealth building is a process.

Final Thoughts

Building wealth is only half the battle. Protecting it and transferring it correctly is where legacy begins.
Too many of our families have lost homes, land, businesses, and hard-earned savings simply because there was no trust in place.
A trust is not just for the wealthy. It's for the wise.
It's the difference between your assets being passed on with

intention, versus being fought over, taxed away, or tied up in court. Every Black family that wants to protect its assets, prevent chaos, and preserve generational wealth needs one. It ensures your family receives exactly what you intend without court interference, delays, or disputes.

Even if you don't have a huge estate, you deserve a plan, structure, and the intention to protect the legacy that you're building.

A TRUST is the key.

CONCLUSION

The Legacy is Yours Now

The Wealth Stack isn't just a financial strategy, it's a cultural shift. This is how we protect our families, reclaim our value, and repair the horrific history behind life insurance.... One policy at a time.

Whether you're starting with $25/month or $25,000/month, what matters most is that you **start.**

History has already shown that we have been excluded from land ownership, capital markets, and business financing. Fortunately now, life insurance is an area where we can now move powerfully and independently.

We're clear that the wealth gap was designed.
So we must task ourselves with the responsibility of eradicating the margin with education, protection, and intention. Life insurance is not a fix-all, but it is one of the most predictable,

affordable, and underused tools for building generational wealth, PERIOD. AND IT'S RISK-FREE.

It's your time to put an end to the generational patterns.
Document your goals.
Have the hard conversations.
And insure your last name like it's the luxury asset that it truly is.

Remember:

- **Term** covers your big-ticket protection.
- **Index Universal Life** supports your retirement + access to cash.
- **Whole Life + PUA** sets up your long-term investment plays.

Policy One is protection- Two is a plan- Three is a legacy.
Together, they make **The Wealth Stack** *REVOLUTION.*

We've walked through the numbers, the history, the myths, and the mindset, and now you have the BLUEPRINT.

YOUR TIME HAS COME TO CULTIVATE LEGACY…

Closing Acknowledgements

To GOD - THE GREATEST TO EVER DO IT! I am, because YOU are.

To my parents, grandparents, and my family- thank you for loving me, caring for me, and making me feel like I was a big deal even when I was just a rooty poot running around, trying to figure life out. You saw the future in me long before I could see it for myself.

To my Ancestors- the ones who survived the unthinkable, who were told "no", even when they were the most qualified in the room. Hell, most times they were the ones who built the room- But I digress… You are the blueprint, the original architects, full of brilliance and resilience- holding humor, dignity and love, in the hard times. Every page of this book is stitched with your strength. Every strategy in these chapters is a love letter back to you. ~We gon' be alright.

To my Woo- Even in your absence, you're still growing me. I love you with my whole heart, and I wish you all of the goodness, love, protection and peace that you've always deserved. I'll never forget the way you've shaped my life. Bless your heart.

To my mentors, friends and extended family- Thank you for showing up when I needed you, for holding me up when I couldn't stand, and for keeping me laughing when crying felt like the only option. You've made the journey lighter, richer, and infinitely more fun. You're the family that I've had the pleasure to choose!

To the reader and buyer- Thank you!

This book and all my prayers are dedicated to better days to come for us all.

Want More?

If this book lit a fire in you know that we're only getting started. Let's stay connected and protected as we grow together.

Work With Yvette B:

1:1 Legacy Strategy Session
Get Life Insurance Now
Life Insurance 101 Group Classes
Speaking Engagements + Brand Partnerships + Appearances

Email: ybm@yvettemotivates.com
Website: www.YvetteBMotivates.com
Instagram: YvetteBMotivates
TikTok: FinanceFashionFlySHT

Published by **YBM PRODUCTIONS LLC**
ISBN - 979-8-89217-682-8

www.ingramcontent.com/pod-product-compliance
Ingram Content Group UK Ltd.
Pitfield, Milton Keynes, MK11 3LW, UK
UKHW022018041026
15591UKWH00012B/367

9 798892 176828